TUMBLING OVER THE EDGE

- a rant for children's play

by BEV BOS & JENNY CHAPMAN

Tumbling Over the Edge - a rant for children's play

Text copyright © Beverley J. Bos and Jennifer Chapman, 2005
Illustrations copyright © Michael Leeman, 2005

www.turnthepage.com

Edited by Michael Leeman.
Design and Graphics by Michael L. Bos.

Printed by Finishline - Print Specialist
Shingle Springs, CA (916) 933-3351

ISBN: 0-931793-02-5

Photos (pages 106, 108, 147, 157) copyright © 2005
Picturemonster.com, PO Box 352 Roseville, CA 95678

All other photos courtesy Bev Bos and Jenny Chapman.

Special thanks to Maggie Schmidt and Sue Fraser.
                                        - B. B. & J. C.

"Old friends cannot be created out of hand. Nothing can match the treasure of common memories, of trials endured together, of quarrels and reconciliations and generous emotions. It is idle, having planted an acorn in the morning, to expect that afternoon to sit in the shade of the oak."

- Antoine de Saint-Exupery

Tumbling Over the Edge
- a rant for children's play

Table of Contents -

PREFACE FOR THE READER

This is a rant for children's play. It is a book about the play environment for young children in their homes, schools, childcare facilities and gathering places. We invite you, while exploring this text, to reconnect with the experiences of your own childhood: the smells, the feelings, the tastes, the touches, the anxieties, the sadnesses, the thrills, the spills, the clandestine activities, the fun of play and the experiences of life and of death. It is our intent to focus your attention upon the importance of childhood play and its relevancy for human growth.

Children have many needs that must be met within a family setting, whether the family is biologically or socially constructed. Critical to the early life of a youngster, along with food, shelter and clothing, is the need to belong to a family, then to a neighborhood and then to a community. Humans possess a social fragility, which can be devastating without the ongoing bond to other humans. In most of our cities, towns and even villages people live lives of endless mobility. They rarely stay in one community for a lifetime and thus there is an absence of kin and close friends for millions of people.

Belonging for young children is being in a place where they feel comfortable enough to play without having to look over their shoulders seeking approval – or dodging disapproval – to explore without fear, to redefine their space and to use materials found around them to create for themselves a sense of order, pattern and structure.

In a place of belonging, a haven, children have people who know without words when they need to be held, that they need to be listened to, cared for and loved unconditionally. Children know when they are accepted and when their play needs are understood. And certainly when they are not.

Play for young children is the most powerful stimulus which initiates discovery of their world. The human infant is born with the drive to explore, discover and to make personal order of its surroundings.

We make no apology for our insistence that in our opinion many young children and their families are living lives enmeshed in pressures that are detrimental to healthy growth and contentment.

- Bev Bos and
Jenny Chapman

The conventional wisdom in child development divides growth into four areas: intellectual, social, emotional and physical . These four areas of development impact the play of young children.

Intellectual development and the skills of reading, writing and arithmetic are areas, which cause parents and politicians to fret and fume over the apparent regression of each generation. Many harangue the school systems and are obsessed with test scores and early achievement profiles. These obsessions are meaningless and counter-productive. It is the ability to relate to others, to work as a group, to problem-solve and our intellectual strengths that support humanity in its ongoing romp on this earth.

Socially, very young children stay close to a parental figure and, as the days pass, move away from the protection of the adult, ready to face the world upon their own feet. The confidence they display in the wider world has some links to the time when parents and family responded to this child by being there to protect, to carry, to rock, to hold, to watch and to trog around with them.

A major task of childhood is to become socially competent and to start to develop a set of moral and ethical values, which guide one as an adult. These values are best learned in the action and reaction mode of play with other members of the community. They are least effective if the values are lessons in a book or set out as an imposing list of rules.

Every society has a code of behavior that affects emotional development. Young children take their cues from the people around them. If children are not able to read these, and act accordingly, they may become an outcast. When playful, trustworthy, warm and caring adults walk alongside the young, suppressing their own adult needs, they help young children absorb the social codes. These codes are essential for children to enter in and retreat from groups.

"Who signed me up for this?"

This is the basis of social survival. When young children understand these codes they are able to communicate their emotional needs without hurting others or submitting to the group's demands under threat. Children who have been supported by adults in negotiating and deferring gratification are often more socially adept.

Physically, young children appear to be in perpetual motion and constantly striving first to be a crawler, then a walker and by four years of age, a runner. Scope for the runner is limited in many places where children spend time. Far too many children are often prevented from running. This moving is seen as an infringement of an adult's control. Play space should be set up so that all physical stages can be accomplished and honored.

Children at play repeatedly pretend and role-play numerous situations, which reflect the family, the home, the school and the media. We are distressed that television characters may carry more weight in children's growing years that their family, friends and relatives. The question parents need to pose is: Whose values do they want their children

"2 cups sand, 3 pebbles, one hand full of flower petals, then add water."

to grow up with? Is it the values of the TV advertisers, scriptwriters, fictitious TV characters or people directly connected to their children's world, their teachers, friends or family?

Play is the finest conduit that we have to develop divergent thinkers. All the intellectual giants have been problem solvers whether they were out on the horizon of physics or in the midst of a search for historical theory. Today, the people who tussle with computer programs or wield a wrench to fix ailing cars are all using advanced problem solving techniques.

A characteristic of curious, creative people is the predisposition to do things in different ways. Sometimes creativity is profit driven, as in our economy, or necessity driven, as in the use of an aluminum can to fashion a washer to fix a machine. Scientific and artistic progress would shrink, shrivel and stagnate without a constant infusion of new ideas spawned by play-driven learners.

We are reminded of the story of Edison's search for the ideal material to use as the filament in his light bulb. He tested no fewer than 6,000 vegetable compounds. His lack of a formal education certainly did not interfere with his genius, the ability to "play around with an idea."

"Is this alive?"

In the midst of play, with its apparent disorder, chaos and mess, is a very deep-seated drive to establish order which makes sense to the young child. Children may persist at one activity for a long time or they may flit from one action to another with apparent random energy. Adults may interpret this behavior as a waste of time. They feel this time could be more profitably used in formal, teacher-directed instruction in the mastery of reading, writing and arithmetic skills. However, attempts to divert children from their self-directed play shuts down the drive to explore and to experiment. These two prongs, exploration and experimentation, are essential to the learning process and have been the roots of all culture – material, spiritual, written and oral – since the beginning of mankind's time upon Earth. They may well be the springboard to future journeys in other realms.

You can learn more about a person
in an hour of play than in a
year of conversation.
*   - Plato*

PREFACE FROM THE AUTHORS

Thirty years of working and paying attention to young children and their families has nudged the two of us to express our concern about environments for childhood. Have we gone too far past remembering how to care for our young children? Have we tumbled over the edge? Children are spending their early years in habitats designed for adults instead of spaces or places that honor and respect the needs of growing, learning, exploring children. Cities, towns, houses, condos, apartments, parks, streets, malls, schools and most public places are planned and built for adults. The needs of children are sacrificed. Get down on your knees and move around and you can appreciate how inhospitable many spaces are for children. Some "state-of-the-art" buildings, even schools prepared for young children, are often institutional rather than aesthetically warm, welcoming places. The space may contain an over-abundance of manufactured toys and commercial materials but lack the basics required for children's exploration. These basics have always been natural materials such as earth, water, wood, clay and sticks and stones and elephant bones.

It seems to us that the division between childhood and adulthood has tragically blurred. This blurring means that the time and space in which small children can play, unfettered by the demands of the adult world, is disappearing.

Childhood as a distinct stage of development has not been present throughout history. The infant-child of the human species has always needed prolonged attention before it was able to be self-sufficient. Only in very recent times have children and childhood been set apart from adults and adult life.

Following the invention of the press, and the beginning of a culture, in which print was accessible to an increasing number of people, it was discovered that a period of time was necessary in which to learn to read. The process of becoming literate, learning to read, highlighted the difference in the brains of

. . . the basics required for children's exploration . . . have always been natural materials such as earth, water, wood, clay, sticks and stones and elephant bones.

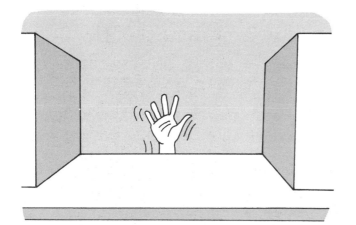

Get down on your knees and move around and you can appreciate how inhospitable many spaces are for children.

Geologists, earthmovers, gardeners, climbers, mountaineers . . .

young children as opposed to the adult brain. We learned that children reached the age of approximately eight before they could learn to read. Childhood, as a unique time in human growth, was acknowledged.

Now at the beginning of the twenty-first century the gap is closing between adulthood and childhood. With this change comes the erosion of time for children to play. It is now common to hurry children into adulthood, and thereby diminish the importance of play in childhood.

Sadly, the media focuses our attention on places that look glossy, unreal, unlived in, cold and smart, but totally lacking any "soul" or warmth. One needs only to look around neighborhoods or cities to see how these pictures influence us in our choices of environments for young children. These spaces and places lack provisions for children to explore, to play and to connect with the natural world.

"Sorry, Kevin, I can't play tag right now, but maybe we can get together and do snack later."

In many schools and programs for young children the adult agenda dominates. Children are told when to go outside, when to eat, when to sleep and how to walk, creating an environment in which the time allowed for playing and "being" a child is marginal. Not only are they told how to walk, but also they must walk "quietly" and use inside voices (what is an inside voice?!?). Children, instead of spending their time playing, now have calendars of commitments, with absolutely no time just to be themselves or even to experience a few precious moments of solitude.

Play sustains children's inborn curiosity while they manipulate and change their surroundings. When children roll balls back and forth against the wall they are becoming aware of cause and effect. This is basic physics. When they are making mud pies or mixing flour and water they are discovering chemistry. When they hum, twirl and spin, the patterns for music, song, dance, reading and mathematics are being laid down in their brains. Children cannot develop into courageous, caring, curious, creative and competent decision makers if they are starved of environments that engage and challenge them. If the children's experience is limited and impoverished, their whole development will be stunted.

More than ever, we have become too constrained by the formalities, rules and expectations of "schooling." Time and attention must be given to transform homes, schools and community environments into spaces having atmosphere, spirit, aliveness, challenges and authenticity. Children are enrolled in formal music lessons, computer skills camps, organized sports and gymnastics before their minds and bodies are ready to accept such disciplines.

We must advocate for places where children wonder, discover, imagine, construct and learn by trial and error so that from their experiences they can develop their own framework of knowledge and a firm sense of self. We hope to strengthen your commitment to children and to support their right to play.

So many of the visitors to the preschool have asked, "What are the rules here?" So, we decided to put them up. Here they are.

The School Rules
For Children:

Run	*Saw*	*Play*	*Follow*
Jump	*Hammer*	*Be Alone*	*Watch*
Dig	*Paint*	*Examine*	*Hear*
Explore	*Ride*	*Experiment*	*Smell*
Talk	*Imagine*	*Express*	*Taste*
Build	*Sing*	*emotions*	*Mix*
Tear Down	*Wonder*	*Touch*	*Create*
Pour	*Measure*	*Work*	*Daydream*
Yell	*Ponder*	*Lead*	*_ _ _ _ _ ?*

The School Rules
For Adults:

Listen
Observe
Be prepared to "step in" with guidance when a child is on the verge of:
* *Hurting Themselves* • *Hurting Another Child*
* *Destroying Property*

I have a garden of my own,
Shining with flowers of every hue,
I loved it dearly while alone,
But shall love it more with you.
- Thomas Moore

Chapter One

THE ROSEVILLE COMMUNITY PRESCHOOL

A Philosophical Statement -- Bev

I realize that in my work with young children, I have moved beyond the stage of providing a daily program which captivates children and satisfies parents, to having developed a deep appreciation of the many ways in which small children learn. I have learned to trust my observation that children require considerably more time, space and materials than most adults allow. Young children are driven by curiosity and a need to explore and experiment with everything around them. This time in their lives is just a whisper, a brief moment, in which they can enjoy the richness of a childhood space.

My task, in the preschool environment, is that of planner, custodian, consultant, scrounger, inventor, play partner and gatherer who provides riches such as scarves, wheels, shovels, hoses, buckets, old shoes, pieces of wood, blocks and art materials. Much more attention is given to the basics: sand, dirt, water, blocks, paint and the need to move and to explore. Then, in conjunction with co-teachers, parents and children, I orchestrate the emotional, physical, social and intellectual climate in the school. My responsibility is to provide

My task . . . is that of planner, custodian, consultant, scrounger, inventor, play partner and gatherer

This time in their lives is just a whisper, a brief moment, in which they can enjoy the richness of a childhood space.

the structure, the materials, the security, the trust and most of all the time to support play.

Jenny recalls her impressions following her first visit to the Roseville Community Preschool in 1993 and during a return visit in 1998.

I was fascinated to find a preschool with indoor and outdoor space that was, and still is, very different from preschools elsewhere. Why is this school different? It is different because children have freedom to become totally engrossed in play with water, ice, sand, paint, wood and words. Time for wonder and exploring are foremost in the ways the teachers support the children. I always come away from this place with a feeling that it is unique and could be an example of the kind of surroundings in which children could thrive, grow and carry with them the strength of who they are. The strong sense of self that they develop, I believe, will be part of their core for life.

ROSEVILLE SCHOOL -- SPRING 1993

Open the door and the air of a warm California spring afternoon floats towards the senses. The visual impact of colorful space dances before the eyes: the floor paint spiraling in all directions; chairs in reds, blues, greens and yellows that are decorated in free-form patterns; the parents' gift from a work weekend and the round tables awaiting action. The bubbles dance in the fish tank and the snake is coiled around the oily looking black branches in the terrarium. One loft houses boxes of manipulative toys and a Plexiglas floor window to check or spy upon the people down below. Across the cargo-net bridge, enclosed and wobbly, is the second loft, which houses a child size room containing miniature beds, a stove, a refrigerator, a table, chairs, dolls (clothed and unclothed), books and cooking utensils. Most importantly, bits of

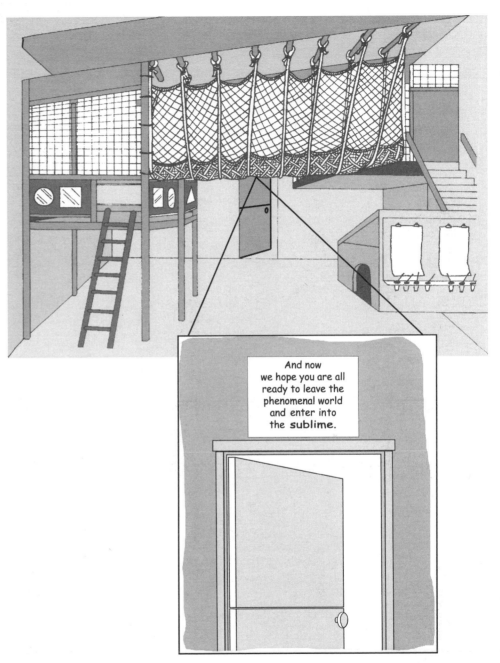

And now we hope you are all ready to leave the phenomenal world and enter into the sublime.

Sign over the door leading to the outside of the Roseville Community Preschool.

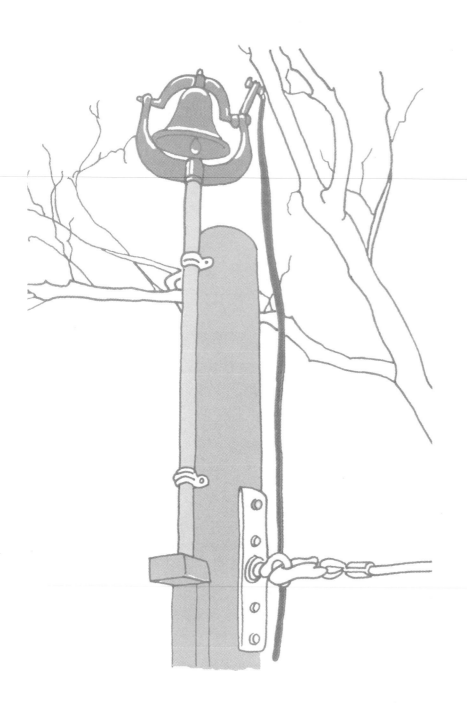

pieces of gathered stuff (flowers, clay, rocks, paper, play dough, seeds) are strewn about – a child's ingredients for imaginative play.

Below there is a carpet of colored squares, a rocking chair and books and puzzles in abundance. Musical instruments and sound makers are gathered in baskets. The latest inventions of copper pipes balanced upon insulation tube to mimic a xylophone and fishing line fastened on mini harps waiting to be twanged are on a table.

Open the back door leading to the yard where well-worn tables – which have withstood the pounding of hammers, splotches of paint, clay and water – stand firmly rooted in the sand. The path curves around the metal spaceship structure and ropes hang inert from branches. A high structure with three levels intertwines with the trees. The walls have wire mesh for safety but the platforms still provide a place to experience the power of being high up and to survey the world from above.

Images of lookouts and of princesses in towers flood into the mind. The trees are just coming into leaf and the daffodils in the garden patch are opening. Buckets, spades, pipes, hoses, trucks, tubes, tubs and gutter – all the props needed for sand and water play – are stored snugly against the red painted sides of the building. The clouds hover as thin wisps in the blue sky, sunlight bouncing off the tree branches.

Back inside, I was told to "try this, it is the best thing we do." It is squeegee painting, where blobs of tempera paint are drawn across paper with a window-cleaning squeegee. One can also mess about with the sound makers, the coffee can thumpers and pitch bottles. But the best of all is not the sound makers or the squeegee painting, but the magnetic paper clip and string which is held in a horizontal position. The challenge is to keep the horizontal string in tension. This provides the adults with another "what will happen if?" as they prepare for the children's return Monday morning.

On Sundays, preparing for Mondays, Bev often looks for and plays with new materials or tries to find new ways for the children to use old ones. That passion and commitment is in some ways mesmerizing. Bev's energy could be daunting for a lesser mortal, but perhaps her energy is a catalyst to help one push out at the edges of creative play. How impressive the changes in education might be if each child entered a room on Monday morning where the passion and energy of a teacher had exploded like a firework, constantly seeking to find other ways of seeing, touching, tasting, smelling and hearing! A classroom should be a place where to be creative with your hands; your intellect or your heart is honored.

It's Monday morning and the children arrive, some with a rush and some wandering about to find a space, a friend and an opportunity to explore. The play begins. Coffee and a snack for the parents are set out. Children can have their favorite snack – crackers – if they are hungry. People congregate in the small office, which accommodates Carrie, the school manager, and the phone, stove, copy machine and sink. This is the place where people gather to swap news and views, and share their triumphs and frustrations.

More children arrive with parent helpers. Visitors arrive for the session; there are often about six a day. Many visitors look around puzzled, some are awed by what is going on, others are animated, others are unsure of what is happening. Play unleashes the energy as the doing, grouping, regrouping, laughing, messing, running, swinging, nibbling and connecting gets underway. There is no teacher's voice controlling and directing here, just the occasional word of encouragement and the sharing of an

There is no teacher's voice controlling and directing here, just the occasional word of encouragement and the sharing of an idea, a dialogue, a conversation, a scribed story or songs.

idea, a dialogue, a conversation, a scribed story or songs.

Parents fan out with clipboards. They are waiting for an opening to present itself for a conversation with a child. They ask, "How does your story start?" Some children enter into the process while others shrug off the invitation. (Maybe later, or another day?) There is always time.

Outside there are stones, sand, pipettes, food color and water to combine and explore, pour, mold and change. The children's concentration is intense. Others scoot around on tricycles and climb into the forts or swing on ropes, each time testing and maximizing their own level of competence. In the dress up room a drama is being played out. It may spill out into the yard but now the children have the door firmly shut.

The art area is busy. The scrapers* are at work but then children begin to make handprints and paint all over the table. Soon finger paint covers the table with a peach-colored paint slick; nails and fingers etch scratchy patterns around and around. Then a child tries printing with her upper torso. A little later, rags appear on the table and all hands help to wash off the tabletops. The children go into the bathroom; they strip off their dirty clothes and find dry, all unaided by adults. These children know that their actions are accepted and the power is in their hands.

It's group time and some children gather for a song, a story, books (if the book chosen does not engage the children on the first few pages it is put down and another book is taken from the stack), a conversation, a dance or a game. Children and adults cluster together to move, talk, sing, dance and listen.

Snack time is a celebration akin to a noisy family dinner. There is lots of time to talk and eat. Then it is off to the carpeted area where the basket full of home stuff waits

Storytelling process: How does your story start?

and, if children have brought something from home, they find it and show it to someone else. Now there is another buzz of children's voices in conversation.

The children then finally leave for home. Farewell! Grab a broom; it is time to sweep again. There is some cleaning up and sorting to be done which adults do gracefully. Real play has happened today and the parents here appreciate that their children are involved in a process of play that is bait for future learning.

ROSEVILLE SCHOOL -- SPRING 1998

Five years later the spirit of the place is still intact. Children and their play requirements are central in the planning but there have been major changes to the yard. It has undergone a renaissance, for the space outside is now evolving into a garden. It is a reminder for me that the play space must never be considered finished.

Transformations, additions, destructions, changes, rebuilding and reseeding are happening here. Children should feel free to move, modify and adapt the space to their play. The inside space still provides opportunities for children to delve into art, science, music, language, building, constructing, moving and make-believe. The richness of the materials makes them appealing and accessible to the children. The interactions with the materials encourage immersion in the basics of wonder, discovery and experimentation.

Outside, through the door into the yard, the scene has changed. A green and growing garden has been woven into the play space.

The high fort structure has been demolished but the platforms in the tree are still there. A room for mechanical things has been built on one side of the yard. It has a loft

Hammering roofing nails into palm stumps.

high up for solitude or escape. There is a ship structure with ladders and platforms, a mast, a wheel, a sail, ropes and pulleys. This is a perfect place for pirates and a space from which to repel all unwanted boarders.

The massive sand pile has become the heart and lungs of this yard. Water pulsates into the rivers and trenches, which emerge after children dig with tough child-size shovels. Gutter, lumber, rocks and loose parts* are used in endless dam construction which captures the attention of children from toddlers to teens. Problem solving abounds and the plans made and remade show the value of the elements of sand and water. They are of central importance in childhood spaces. Adults, at least the pre-television, pre-Nintendo generation, when asked to go back in memory, nearly always remember unfettered play like this in rural and urban spaces.

The ingenuity in this greening project is that the planting has not impinged on the space for running, digging, flooding, riding, chasing, engineering or climbing. On the contrary, it has added many more options for everything that happens inside to happen outside. Plant-screened places may become a playhouse, store, hospital or office. There is room to use paint on the art lathe, fences or tables. There are spaces to sit and to read books and there is always room for dramatic play and dress up.

Sand has migrated inside, not in a sand table but heaped upon a table six inches from the ground and tucked under the loft. Blocks which once held a prime place in the block room are now stacked in milk crates along a wall with another miniature table. These form a solid base for a multitude of towers and structures built with an expanding variety of blocks: brought, found and scrounged. Watch children and they will use everything for building.

Gatherings and clumpings of children still happen for stories, story plays, dancing and singing, but snack time has changed. One parent helper sets up snack at a table and some children may choose to assist the adult in chopping, stirring, cracking eggs, scrambling, spreading and arranging food on plates. Children come when they feel the need to sit and eat. More attention can be given to conversing with an individual child than to a group at snack time with the inevitable crossfire of serving, spills, demands and chatter. Here is a golden opportunity to develop deeper bonds with individual children.

There is a patina upon this place with its well-worn wooden tables with crooked legs braced to keep them firm and a rocking boat (rarely used for rocking). The ceramic bowls are filled with treasured rocks collected from near and far, each with a story to tell of a granite slide, a volcanic fire or a tumbling wave action. The tile mosaic is plastered upon a shed wall behind the spring garden where the seedling sunflowers begin their yearly journey towards the sun. All of this contributes to making this nirvana for children.

What makes this childhood domain always the same yet constantly renewing its form is the energy and hard work of creative adults which pulls one generation along into the adventure of passionate, productive play.

Today the energy expressed itself in the construction of a waterfall, made with a cube of PVC pipe drilled with holes and a hose. The children were diffident at first, but then warmed up to the invitation to get totally, drippingly, clingingly WET shirts, socks, shoes, pants and dresses as they played with sheer delight with the water and pipe. I could not help but feel a deep sadness that more children, in the midst of their precious childhood years, were not given the chance to enjoy such simple time-tested pleasures.

12

Chapter Two

"AND WHEN ARE YOU GOING TO BAKE BREAD?"

Jenny

The children were absorbed cramming wheat berries into a hand-cranked grinder and cranking it relentlessly. I watched this for a while as the pile of flour mounted beneath the grinder. Bev walked by and I asked, innocently enough, *"And when are you going to bake bread?"* "In about three months," was the reply.

It was a whack on the side of the head and truly made me rethink everything we do in many early childhood programs. I was used to seeing in many classrooms the bread making begin with the mixing of flour, yeast, salt and water. It would continue with the cooking stage, followed by eating and finishing with the telling of the old folktale *The Little Red Hen* that is often embraced as a *fine* thematic unit.

Bev

The following is my reply to Jenny's original question: *"And when are you going to bake bread?"*

The school has a plethora of juicers, grinders, mashers and ricers. Whether children like juice or not does not make any difference to the amount of time and energy they spend juicing, grinding and mashing. What I notice is that adults often do not understand that for young children it is the process that is

"Childhood is the world of miracle and wonder, as if creation rose and bathed in light, out of the darkness, utterly new and fresh and astonishing. The end of childhood is when things cease to astonish us. When the world seems familiar, when we have got used to existence, one has become an adult."

- E. Ionesco

Fascination with flow.

Fruits of labor.

important. It is the grinding, the cranking of the handle and seeing the juice spurt out, not the drinking of the juice or the making of the bread. Sometimes when visiting adults ask questions, I respond with my heart, not my brain. I was honestly stunned when Jenny walked away. It was days before we returned to the question "*And when are you going to bake bread?*"

For threescore years and ten, children have always made mud pies: mixing, stirring, pouring, patting and baking confections in the sun. Even when part of a child's day was spent cooking and helping prepare the meals for their families, children still played at making pretend food for friends and pets.

In some classrooms for young children, the adult-driven plan will provide for an experience such as making bread. "Today, we are going to make bread," they say, and sure enough the flour, yeast, sugar, salt, water, spoons, measuring cups, bowls and aprons are dished out to the chosen participants. Bread is dutifully made, cooked and eaten. The climax for the day will be the reading or the telling of the folktale, *The Little Red Hen*. While in the past I have told this same story, I have come to know that it represents a pressure, however subtle, by telling children you do not eat if you do not work.

Another constraint that disregards the developmental process is the teaspoon-of-everything approach to making bread or biscuits or whatever. It is not the bread, biscuits or the eating that is important for the children, but the fifty pounds of flour and water to mix and mix and mix.

Take another tack with this bread baking and step back to the stage of grinding the grain with assorted hand-cranked grinders which, when turned and turned, pulverize the grains into flour. Here is a place for discovery and mastery. Adults concentrate on the end product of baked bread, but

Here is a place for discovery and mastery.

children enjoy the endless action of grinding. It is time to reflect upon the process, not the product.

Before the children come to your place and play, or when you have a small baby in your home, sit down with a piece of paper and pose these two questions to yourself: What is the worst possible outcome of extensive play, mixing, grinding or stirring? What is the optimum outcome? Somewhere in the middle is probably what will happen. If, in your head, a voice says, *"Don't make a mess," "That's too much," "Keep the flour on the table," "Remember you have to clean up,"* or *"That's enough water,"* bury those thoughts and accept that you are their clean-up partner. Now be prepared for an adventure as you assist your young scientist and say, *"I wonder what would happen if . . ."* Young children's curiosity is sustained when their *"Hey, I have an idea!"* and *"I need some more . . ."* are taken seriously.

I asked, *"How long?"* Of course, she replied, *"Till its done."*

<u>Bev and Jenny</u> – Mariah, five years old, started mixing flour and water in a large bowl. She added salt and sand. After using different utensils to mix and stir for an hour or so, she had a smooth mixture to which she added an abundance of food coloring. She asked for a baking pan and we found a small baking pan, but it needed to be bigger. Back to the cupboard we went, and began another search for the *right* pan. Mariah smoothed the batter in the pan and then turned, and handed it to me, asking me to bake it. She *knew* we would support her project. I asked, *"How long?"* Of course, she replied, *" 'Till it's done."* We checked the cake repeatedly until it reached a satisfactory baked state. When we lifted it from the oven it almost fell to the floor. It must have weighed fifteen pounds. We had the grace and dignity to accept a piece and taste it.

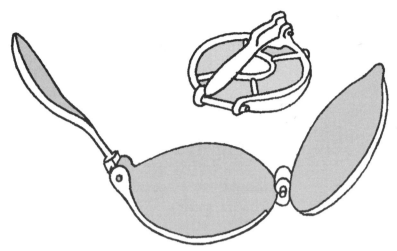

Tortilla presses

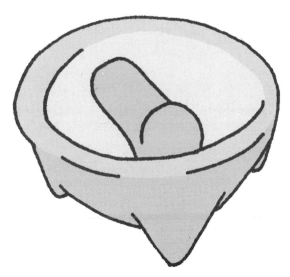

Mortar and pestle

". . . and just a pinch of salt."

The process of mixing, adding and stirring had taken most of the morning. The final stage was converting the mixture into a cake. Chemistry was happening here. Going from wet to dry, additions of salt and sand, then color changes and then returning to a solid state with heat application was all part of the process.

Children love to mix, and we must be ready for it! Sometimes this is difficult for people whose space is limited and their time is short. If you watch children sifting, stirring and mixing you will understand how much time it takes and how satisfying it can be. It takes only a plastic bowl, a spoon, flour and water. A child will play for hours and hours.

Babies, toddlers, children, teenagers, adults and the checkout generation will only be deeply connected to the stream of humanity if they continue to see, touch, taste, smell, hear and feel in their world as if it had just appeared in all its newness, wetness, dryness, lightness, darkness, silence and crescendo of sound.

Think of it this way, if the only apple you have contact with is a plastic look-alike, a flashcard, a computer graphic or

apple

a magazine cutout, then you have missed the pleasure of sourness, sweetness, mushiness, roundness, the texture, the color, the size and shape, the juiciness, the stickiness, the bugs and blemishes, the seeds and the connection to the continuous cycle of life.

"Where is your real work for today?"

<u>Jenny</u> – One morning, in a child care center I was visiting, I noticed a basket of apples on a shelf. Another visitor, an instructor in an early childhood college program, asked if she could share an apple story with a child. The reply was that those apples had been earmarked for the teacher to take home and make into applesauce that night which would be brought back to the center the next day. The college instructor offered to use her own lunch apple for the venture, which involved cutting open the apple and discovering the seeds inside. The child was fascinated by the discovery of the seeds and the dialogue with the adult. The child wanted to save the seeds to show his mother at home, so the seeds and cut apple were put into a container.

When the child's mother came to collect him he ran up to her with intense excitement wanting her to see the cut up apple and the seeds. She gave it a cursory glance, asking, *"Where is your real work for today?"* A scrap of paper was produced with a ditto drawing, hastily scribbled over, to which the mother responded enthusiastically. It saddened me that the real learning that had happened for the child with the apple and seeds that morning was ignored.

We must all find ways of supporting children in their learning. This support can take the form of helping adults recognize and nurture the "seeds" of real learning. The challenge is finding a way to do this without unduly rattling or embarrassing teachers, caregivers and parents. The

Children have got to have too much.

more we practice appropriate ways of standing up for children the more we can champion that behavior for other adults. Then, in an intense moment when we are upset, we will remember what to do. How much better it would have been in the example above, if the teacher had taken three deep breaths and then in a quiet, gentle voice said, *"I would really like to see those apple seeds."* Unfortunately, both the teacher and the parent appeared to be confined to a very narrow appreciation of learning. They were more comfortable with a tangible pencil and paper product representing the child's involvement during the morning rather than taking the risk of going outside the box of convention. The exploration with the apple is a risk with no predetermined outcome; however, before children

can enter the academic kaleidoscope they need to risk involvement in the unknown. They have to be given the freedom to learn, feel, change, grow, love and live. Risk propels us forward and helps us trust ourselves as capable individuals. A child knows this instinctively.

Vats of carrots!

Bev – A child, four years old, was fascinated with the grinder and after a whole morning of turning the crank had produced vats of carrots. After a few days of grinding, the carrots overflowed the table. We moved the grinder outside where the child could grind to his heart's content.

The children ate what they wanted and still we had bushels of ground carrots. Fortunately, we found a friendly neighborhood horse that loved to eat the fruits of the child's labor.

It is always the process for children, the process of moving the muscles, of cause and effect and a sense of great accomplishment. Adults sometimes are concerned that every child will want to grind a bushel of carrots. After thirty years of being with young children I know that is not usually the case and if it were I would act accordingly and provide more carrots.

Sometimes we focus incorrectly on the issue of fairness. Fairness is not everybody having the same, but rather, everyone having what they need. This is especially true during this stage of development, when the child is most egocentric.

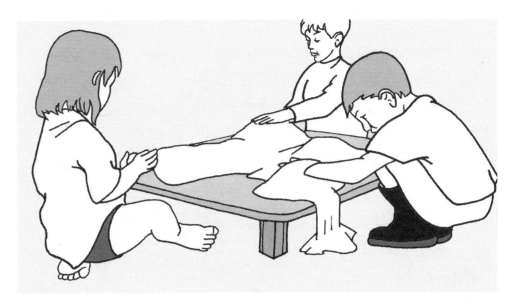

Grinders and juicers of all kinds

No child on earth was ever meant to be ordinary, and you can see it in them, and they know it too, but then the times get to them, and they wear out their brains learning what folks expect, and spend their strength trying to rise over those same folks.

- Annie Dillard

"Come on, you can do it!"

Chapter Three

THE NITTY GRITTY

Belonging • Risk • Passion • Power • Conflict • Limits

Through our experiences with young children and families, we know that certain elements for human growth from infancy to crone hood must be present everyday for robust growth. For children, we, as their caregivers, have the task of creating an environment where all these elements are present.

Belonging

Paramount among these elements is a sense of belonging. Children develop a sense of belonging if they are fed when they are hungry, if they are held, and are kept close to an adult that responds to their physical and emotional needs. Families that have strong intergenerational ties are more likely to provide the stability that young children will need to grow into healthy adulthood. Children belong when adults pay attention to the way they grow and learn and provide the rich natural environment they need.

Signs and lip service that suggest we all belong, that we are all friends, that we are special, or are the person of the month, or are the honor student, are superficial and meaningless with respect to a genuine sense of belonging. It is an internal process. When the child's full range of feelings and emotions, such as fear, anger, sadness, joy, delight, are respected and paid attention to, the child belongs. It is easier for adults to respond to the lighter side of temperament but far more important to reassure and support the child while they cope with painful times.

I walked a mile with Pleasure,
She chatted all the way,
But left me none the wiser,
For all she had to say.

I walked a mile with Sorrow,
And ne'er word said she,
But, oh, the things I learned from her,
When sorrow walked with me.

- Robert Browning Hamilton

Risk

Risk is another element. One must take a chance, stick one's neck out, go through fire and water intellectually, socially, emotionally, physically and spiritually everyday in order to mature. Metaphorically, we use the expression "go through fire and water" to portray the intensity of daring to experience.

To begin with, the baby has to climb a few stairs slowly with a caregiver behind to know how to climb stairs. The crone must keep climbing the stairs to keep the body alive. We must risk making friends and losing friends, and learn to respect difference. We must be brave enough to cry when we are frightened, and to risk involvement by reaching out to help another.

> " . . . a ladder over the ditch -- you can definitely risk a skinned knee here. The message is that I am considered sane and responsible. This is not a padded cell."
>
> - Barry Bussewitz

In each phase of life there are risks to be surmounted. The risk for a baby is different from the risk for a five-year-old. We are the co-players observing, encouraging and watching for new stages.

Passion

We define passion as an intense, emotional drive, a compelling desire to know. It is another element essential for a full life. We are born curious. Watch the faces of children at play: the furrowed brow, the perspiration, the energy, the excitement when the plan works, even the great flow of tears when it doesn't go well. The excitement we feel when our plan works. Interests that begin in childhood

"We've mastered the slide; let's try the stairs."

Egocentric Child

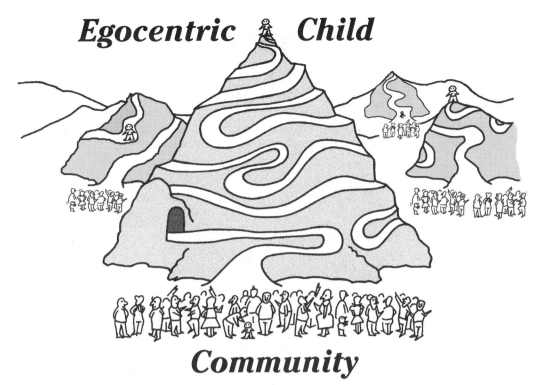

Community

often continue into adulthood. Providing children with a variety of opportunities to play without interference from adults encourages children to further their interests.

Jenny – I know a child who loved to climb and swing and carried on with this passion and interest into adolescence, becoming a talented circus performer and teacher. She had the ability to persist that comes from the length of time she had been encouraged to explore, to use and to develop her talent in her early life.

Bev – Without formal drawing lessons, a young child whose father was an architect would sit and work on intricate drawings way beyond the usual scope of young children. Today she pursues that interest further by continuing the complicated drawings.

Children often display an interest or fascination with an activity. This may be short-term or it may be a long-term passion. Adults aware of this can provide a wide range of experiences, which gives children scope to develop individual talents. The key is to be careful not to narrow the possibilities for children by having preconceived expectations. We must, no matter what inclination the child may appear to have, remain open-minded.

Returning to the circus performer, no one intended that as a child she would become a high-wire artist. At present this is her task, her daily endeavor. In the future, all the multifaceted experiences of honing her performance skills will transfer to other aspects of her life. This "passion followed" sets her up for a life of intensity and discipline.

Power
The responsibility of the adults in a child's world is to provide structure and guidance, which will help the child inch out from the security of the home into the community of school and then further out to the wider community.

"Sometimes I swing, sometimes I swing and write."

The baby is, and rightly so, sitting on top of the mountain, egocentric and self-centered, the pinnacle of the triangle of baby, parent and family. The task of parenting is to bring the baby down the mountain and into the mainstream of humanity.

This means we must pay attention, yet again, to development and to intellectual, social, physical and emotional power. This is not power over others but power with and for others as well as a sense of personal power.

Parents and teachers can help children enormously to continue the journey down the mountain by understanding that children need to have their own power. What this means is that from toddlers to teens you have to gradually let out the thread, which ties the child to the family.

You don't give the keys of the car to a three-year-old or a seven-year-old but, hopefully, by sixteen they have the social maturity and awareness to become a driver. You don't allow the child to dictate what the family will do with its every moment.

What we want for children is power in its most effective form. We want children to have the ability to speak up for themselves without demeaning another person.

Children are given appropriate opportunities for power in the Roseville Community Preschool environment. As you read the following pages, remember that the needs of young children don't change regardless of where they are, whether in homes, schools or child care centers.

As the children come into the school they have the immediate power to choose whether to stay inside or go directly outside. They have power to come in running and run as hard and as long as they need to all morning. When school first starts sometimes the child is hesitant

"It's important to have the right tool for the job."

about when to come in or go out, not knowing they have the choice. By October, however, they just wave hello as they tramp through to their desired destination. There is tremendous power in choosing where you will play, rain or shine. There is power in painting as many pictures as you need to paint, whether it be just one or seventeen.

The same philosophy of power is expressed in our adoption of an informal snack time. Snack is available when children are hungry. Some of our children need to eat the first thing in the morning and occasionally; some may choose not to eat at all. In other words, the children at our school take responsibility for their own hunger. Sometimes they choose to just sit and talk. Sometimes when a child is totally involved in bridge building and engineering, I will take a bowl of hot soup to the laboring child to accommodate and fuel their intense task.

It reminds me of my time on my uncle's farm when we took food to the harvesters. If you have ever seen the look on a hardworking, hungry person's face, then you will understand that it is the right thing to do. At our school, no one would insist that a child eat or drink because doing so would be a complete disregard for the child's decision-making ability. When a child is totally engrossed, mentally and physically, we take care not to interrupt their play.

Respecting a child's play space is also a part of power. The children can build with blocks as high as they wish and are not restricted to knee height or shoulder height construction. There is even greater power in being able to return to your building the next day and add to the structure. We must develop a sense for what is chaos (what needs to be cleaned up) and that, which is part of a child's work.

Water, water, everywhere, nor any drop to drink.
- Samuel Taylor Coleridge

Similarly, when a story is being told or a book being read, the children have the power to add their words, to question what is happening, to interrupt and to clarify. They also have the power to choose to come to story time or not.

Opportunities for power are not limited to the inside spaces. Slides need to be wide enough for two-way traffic. And tricycle paths should not have arrows directing traffic. The power is in decision-making: to go up, or down, left or right, or perhaps even to wait.

Everyday the children play avidly in the large sand, dirt and water area building their own version of the Amazon, London Bridge or perhaps pretend to be digging to China. Here the hose is the most accessible play prop for children. They have sand under foot and a hose in hand, augmented with good shovels, tough ones that really dig. Water from the hose form rivers and dams are built. Some water

escapes and some is absorbed. There is erosion and water saturates the sand. Bikers speed through the overflow on the bike path and children swing over it. Places for the rope swings, hanging from trees and a swing disc, invite Tarzan tactics. Food coloring is added to the water and the Red River flows. Feet, bellies and butts get wet. Children, contrary to some people's beliefs, do not melt but their spirits may well shrivel without the fun and challenge of taming the spouting hose.

If children grow up without a sense of personal power they will be vulnerable. By that, we mean they will be unable to resist forces that are anti-life. Without a sense of personal power one cannot swim against the tide of peer pressure or resist questionable conventions and cannot know the truth for themselves.

Conflict / Limits

The most amazing thing in this space is that the hoses are used to flood the ponds, to flush out the river and to create water for a dam and rarely to soak someone else. There is minimal conflict in this place; inside or outside. Conflict is often the product of the lack of freedom in a controlling environment and the competition for the few meager choices made available to children. Children here are not restricted to the teacher's agenda, the plan for the month or the activity for the day. Again, when a child enters through the door and can immediately go outside to find the digging equipment, the freedom to make a choice is there. This is opposite of the experience of children who are made to sit on a rug, chair or floor until everyone is assembled for the opening song or gathering and then presented with the choice of activity for the day, with words such as, "Today you can choose housekeeping, blocks or the swings."

The goals which we have to assist children in their learning and growing wiser are built into the social as well as physical realm of the preschool. Conflict is bound to occur whenever you have young children in close proximity to each other no matter what environment they find themselves in. This is the reality we must accept. Try not to sabotage the opportunity for children to grow socially with your distractions or premature interference.

There are limits in the Roseville Community Preschool, but people often miss seeing them because the limits are embedded in the environment and are not obvious or posted on charts or shouted at children by over-controlling adults.

The adults in the child's world need to set boundaries. And the reason for this is that it gives the child a feeling of security and safety. When those boundaries are woven into the environment the children are given the courage, often non-verbally, to explore. We put fences up so children

The basics for young children are wonder, discovery, and experience.

- Bev Bos

cannot go in the street and we do not put knives out for them to play with. Electrical outlets must be protected from exploring fingers and forks. When you have a crawling baby and a straight flight of stairs you need a barricade. The baby does not understand stairs yet; they need supervision while mastering stair climbing. Again, we must not abdicate our responsibility to our children. We need to recognize that children need to move, run about, be loud and other activities that don't fit well in adult oriented places like the fancy restaurant, grocery store, long commutes, and most public events. Parents need to know the tolerance level of their children.

"This could be better."

Bev – Six children crowded around the "new" gecko's cage. They were so excited that they pushed each other to see the gecko eat his feast of crickets. Immediately I thought, "This could be better." We must, at least temporarily, move the gecko tank out into the middle of the room so children can get around all sides.

Notice that the adult changed the location of the cage to make it easier for the children to stay connected to the point of interest, the gecko, without having to push and shove or wait in line for a turn, which would break their concentration. As an adult we understand that the gecko will be there tomorrow. However, young children live in the present moment because of their innate curiosity and drive to know. Pay attention to having your children's environment challenging but not dangerous. Adults who focus solely on control and try to dominate the actions of children have lost their own sense of wonder, discovery and exploration.

Fences not only provide boundaries but also furnish places for vines and creepers and make possible the creation of greened spaces.

A retaining wall around a designated area contains the sand, water, shovels and digging activities and prevents them from conflicting with other activities.

There should be many little places (nooks and crannies) for children to play in where they will not be disturbed by others. The space provides the limit. Children will then figure out how many people fit in a space and whether they want to stay there or not.

Two-wheelers are not stable enough for small children. Even with training wheels they can be lethal for children under six. Children cannot focus on two things at once. They might be able to balance and pedal but to be expected to look out for objects in their way is too difficult. Our tricycles, with their fat tires and broad axles, provide a safe, fast ride because they are stable.

Children's troubles and squabbles are diminished when there are enough of the most desirable playthings to go around. We don't have one shovel, but we have at least ten shovels, many buckets, lots of sand and many, many water containers, funnels and pieces of gutter and bamboo troughs and PVC pipe (loose parts).

When adults stand closer to potential trouble spots, not intruding, but watching and keeping quiet, they send a subliminal message to children to cool it.

The woodwork table is twelve feet long and three feet wide - long enough for many children to work side by side. When the space is organized in a child friendly manner, it cuts down the need for excessive supervision, which can drain the energy of parents and teachers. The sense of adventure and wonder is alive if adults are freed from the constant distraction of trying to control children's movement and dampen their enthusiasm. Some of the ways we do this are described below.

Heaps of playdough and not a cookie cutter in sight.

On the tricycle path that could invite speedy trike riding we installed mini wooden ramps that slow down the traffic and they set the speed limit. They are barely six inches at the hump of the bridge but it is interesting to watch young children struggle to pedal up and over the ramps.

There are enough adults in the schoolyard so that children can be where they need to be instead of being where the adults need them to be. The same approach should be used in neighborhoods, homes, childcare facilities or any place that invites exploration. The adult needs to tagalong and pay attention. The child is the explorer. They would rather be outside than inside regardless of the weather. So thought must be given to providing a sheltered outdoor space for use in pouring rain, blinding snow or blistering sun. The limit here lies in not keeping the child cooped up and inside but in adjusting the outside space to accommodate children.

It is interesting to note how often businesses manage to offer this to their patrons. Often restaurants, hotels, grocery stores and airports provide covered areas, umbrellas, trees for shade and outdoors heating; our children deserve the same respect and consideration. Children cannot demand these for themselves. A basic principle followed at Roseville Community Preschool is putting the children and their needs first.

Having enough.

<u>Bev</u> – Freshly made play dough was on the table with numerous rollers, tortilla presses, pumpkin knives and a few other bits and pieces (no sign of a cookie cutter!) to press into the play dough. When children are in a place where they are trusted they almost always build upon the basics of previous experience. A few minutes of rolling and poking and cutting and someone adds some sparkling things to the play dough pieces and calls for a cookie sheet for baking. Other children add color and press and poke and demand their own cookie sheet. Soon large amounts of play dough are baking and the children ask for plastic bags in which to take their treasures home. Later the teacher, in the twenty-minute break between classes, has to make another batch of play-dough.

In this environment the adults do not divide up the play prop (play dough) to give each child the same amount but make enough as required. They expand the quantity and thus eradicate the squabbling, which often erupts when there is too little of something.

"Help me cross the street."

<u>Bev</u> – When my grandchildren were young and we went to the store I would say as we got out of the car, "Hold my hand and help me across the street; those cars come so fast they scare me." A few years later when my grandchildren were a little older, they would say, "Oh, Granny, I just figured it out: you were helping us." We need to be there with a gentle, firm hand and with understanding to encourage appropriate action. If the statements are abstract such as "don't fall," "watch out" and "don't get hurt," children become paralyzed and stop thinking. Young children are in the stage of "here and now." When giving young children any direction it must be very specific. They do not think in

the abstract or understand hypothetical phrases such as these.

Directing a child to "look out" could mean just look at something. A more developmentally appropriate way to give the child direction would be to say, "Here comes someone on a tricycle. Move!"

Not too many years ago, as children we lingered around family and home longer. Our time was not spent in public places like malls, restaurants, movie theaters and theme parks.

Children have had to go "public" too soon. Take for example the grocery store, a difficult place for a child. Children see those wide aisles, cookies, candy and big carts to push as an invitation to play. As the adults in charge we know that the fast shopping stop needs to be done solo. However, the trip to the grocery store can be a social and an interactive time between a parent and child when you take time to involve the child in the process. Not "don't touch," "put it back," and/or "we don't need that," but "let's find five bananas." My daughter Julie, when shopping with her babies, would go to the vegetable aisle first and pick out an eggplant or a melon or an onion and let her child hold it during the shopping frenzy.

If you watch your own children and notice how often you have to repeat a direction or an answer, you will begin to understand their development. They are NOT misbehaving; they simply do not understand the concepts. Notice how often when you ask a small child where they got hurt, that they will take you to the scene of the accident rather than show you the injured body part.

What follows are some of the paralyzing statements that undermine the evolution of independence.

You're Just Tired!
Look Out!
Don't Fall!
Stop Running!
Walking Feet!
Don't Get Dirty!
Be Careful!!
You're Not Hurt!
Don't Get Wet!

Be careful!
Look out!
You'll get hurt!
Don't fall!
You will be sorry!
Don't run!
Watch out!
Don't get wet or you will catch a cold!
Oh, you're not hurt!

Any list of responses would be contrived. It is helpful, however, to understand that children remember the last word they hear so if you are going to say, "Watch out," for example, they will just remember "out." If you say "Watch the car," they may focus on the car, especially if you are holding their hand and are standing still yourself until it is safe to cross.

You cannot live life without conflict. It is a disservice to our children to eliminate opportunities to become negotiators. Confused by shattered traditions and searching for immediate solutions, adults are caught up in the vicious circle of trying to change their children instead of changing the conditions that pose the real threat. Adults need the strength to help children develop a civil way of coping with conflict. In settling disputes, an eye for an eye and a tooth for a tooth, does not diminish conflict, nor does abrogating your responsibility to establish reasonable limits avoid conflict.

Bev's niece, a mother of two young children, asked, "If we have all this knowledge about how children grow best why doesn't it change?

It is a disservice to our children to eliminate opportunities to become negotiators. You cannot live life without conflict.

*That pain inside the child
should not linger for
any length of time.*

*You absolutely must understand
the stories will be different.*

We believe that when we are tired, scared, hurried, burdened or just frustrated we react to situations the way our parents did and perhaps, our grandparents. Our parents did the very best they could with the knowledge that they had. Some things our parents did can, and should be passed on, but there are other things parents wished they had not done that should be firmly in the past. It is very difficult to change the patterns of parenting.

Children in play are ready to set the line for others. Instead of turning a blind eye to the anger they express, we can support the child in working through the problem. Young children, in spite of their egocentric nature, can move from a "stand off" to an "inclusive" stance. Our task is to encourage the inclusive stance.

Truthfully, most everyone I know wants his or her own way. Adults need to focus on coping with conflict rather than conflict removal so that healthy and constructive ways of dealing with conflict problems may be practiced in childhood and used the rest of their lives. This is especially true of young children when they are still in the egocentric stage of growth. Discipline needs to be firm, kind and tender. Helping children with this takes precedence over whatever else may be going on. If they are sad, hurt, angry or feeling misunderstood, my goal is to assist children in finding a solution without battering or pushing or hitting one another. We often ask egocentric children to "use their words" before they understand the words or are able to empathize with another person's feelings. At this time in life young children view everything in the world in relation to themselves, for they have to be self-centered as a baby to survive, to scream for food and comfort.

Because young children are so present and immediate, timing is crucial. The pain inside the child should not linger for any length of time whether it is the physical pain of the hurt or the humiliation or embarrassment.

To begin the tiny steps of coping with conflict, here is an example of a confrontation:

Bobby: "Waaaaaahh!"
Me: (Gently touching the child) "Tell me what happened."
Bobby: "She hit me!" (Pointing to arm).
Me: "Can you tell me who hit you?"
Bobby: "Waaaahh, Jane!"
Me: "Do you want Jane's hand on your arm?"
Bobby: "NO!"
Me: "Well, you better go tell Jane 'cause maybe she thinks you do."

What I want for Bobby is POWER; he must be able to tell Jane he doesn't want her to touch him, and tell her in a way that Jane will clearly understand.

"I DON'T WANT YOUR HAND ON MY ARM!"

It is natural to want to be harmonious. When a child is pushing buttons, overstepping limits, hurting others repeatedly, we need to try to find out what is happening in this little person's life, what stresses are present. The behavior could be due to chemical changes and/or growth spurts or perhaps the inconsistencies in the child's life.

Most of us were not encouraged to look for solutions as a child. What parents said was law. In many ways that was the easier way. The teacher, the parent or the adult became the enforcer of the rules and dispenser of punishment. What we want for children is to have the ability to start looking for solutions on their own. The troubling behaviors can become entrenched early and things rarely get better for the child unless adults rally around and strengthen the bonds of attachment so that the child has the mentor, the confidant, the monitor, the protector the person in the child's life that will never give up.

John said stupid and shut up to me and hit me in the face. But I am going to play with him in 6 minutes and then in 7 minutes I will like him again.

That's it,
Kavi

If you close your eyes and think back to a time when you were very angry you can probably remember that whatever anyone else said was just not right. Many of us have driven too fast, vacuumed like a whirlwind or tossed things around when we were very angry. There is a tremendous energy in anger and the first thing we must do with angry children is help them to move in order to release that anger and not confine them to a "time-out chair." In order to bridge the space between conflict and cooperation we need to have ample time to release energy. Running is a good way. Grab them by the hand and head out the door. Run until you can feel that tense little body let down. Then ask, "Can you go back in?" At this point I talk about the incident only if the child starts the conversation. When we go back I try to stay close. One really important thing I keep in mind is that anger is always secondary. Often, children are just hungry, tired or frustrated. Always keep in mind that humiliations can never be undone.

I greet my children at the school door and sometimes I can tell by the look on the child's or the parent's face it has been a difficult morning. Anguish is present. So my intervention starts immediately. Before the children reach the door of the school they have the opportunity to stroll though a labyrinth of rock and flowers and herbs. Or on occasions I have helped a children ease into the day by climbing in their car with them. Sometimes it is so easy. I just listen to the child. Most of all I just try to remember what it was like to be a child and feel out of sorts with others.

When people visit the school they remark on the lack of "discipline problems" and I believe that the environment is one issue. When children are respected and unyielding demands are not made of them, few situations seem hopeless.

When planning I try to think more about individuals and

Water is the very breath of life to a child.

do not give much thought to gender; however I am very aware that boys playing the more active games like chase need the space for running, leaping, jumping, flying, rolling, wrestling, pummeling and play fighting.

It would not be an inaccurate observation that girls tend to spend more time in the art and playhouse areas or the cut and color table and generally play inside. Girls will sit and "natter" to each other.

One point that needs to be considered here is that the vast majority of the environments in which young children spend their days are overseen by women. We witness the tendency in women of not honoring the physicality of boys. All young children, however, will be shortchanged if we fail to understand that children (both boys and girls) need

physically active play. Somewhat blindly, society expects that all boys will fit into the schooling environment that is primarily orchestrated by women.

When a young boy is moving without appearing to pay attention to where he is going, it is not necessarily a behavior problem, but it may be an indication that his nervous system is not fully developed. It is crucial if we want to raise healthy young men and young women – mentally, physically, spiritually and emotionally – that we take the time to find out what a child friendly environment looks like.

Water is the one thing that seems to have more energy than the young child.

Bev – If someone were to challenge me by saying, "What is the one essential every environment for young children should have?" my immediate response, without question, would be water. Water is the very breath of life to a child. It is the most desirable element for encouraging a deep, ongoing relationship with the natural world and fostering intellectual inquiry. Water is difficult to contain which is why the possibilities for experimentation are vast; yet the simple action of pouring and scooping rivets children's attention and demands further exploration. It is soothing and relaxing as the child pours from one container to the next. And at other times it is uncontrollable – as the dam breaks or as the hose does its dance and thrashes around the yard. Water is the one thing that seems to have more

energy than the young child, even an angry child. In water play, children are faced with the task of channeling this omnipotent element in much the same way adults are pushed to find ways to respect the energy of the child without interrupting its flow. Water is the one thing that meets the needs of young children in every way including the "angry energy" of the frustrated child.

Dam busters, mud haulers, sand patters

Bev – In the play yard, there are twenty yards of sand in one big pile. The crater at the top of sand heap has been dug to an approximate depth of two feet. The hose is dragged over to fill the void with water. Children know that if they step in the hole up to their knees, others will follow their lead. Whatever the temperature, children disregard the cold and concentrate on building lakes and dams to contain their water supply. These engineers, dam builders, dam busters, mud haulers and sand patters work together with beaverish intensity to stem the flood and direct the power of the water flow.

A male visitor stood, watching this play. The children called upon him to help them. They could tell by his body language that he was approachable and could be called upon to assist as an additional worker. He has told us that he considers the outside play place at Roseville Community Preschool to be one of the most "boy friendly" environments he has visited. Of course, the space is also girl friendly. The individual biases of a child will draw them towards play opportunities that satisfy their own needs. Boys are not the only ones who play in the water, shovel the sand, dig to China and climb in the trees. It is fair to comment

Mighty Giant Man

that girls are more likely cluster around the cut and color table than the boys between the ages of three to seven. However, when we pay attention to the idiosyncrasies of each child we will ensure that we provide enough scope for individual children to learn in a multitude of ways.

We started this chapter by talking about Belonging, Risk, Passion, Power, Conflict and Limits. The following story of the Mighty Giant Man perfectly illustrates how all these elements come together in the nitty gritty of play.

Jenny – One morning, the side kicking of the karate masters was causing excitement in the tribe of four-year-olds. As they copied the moves, they quickly moved into wrestling mode. A Dad, who was helping in the preschool, saw this and went to the rug area to play the "mighty giant man." With exquisite patience and setting firm limits to stop the play when the unacceptable actions of kicking and chopping were introduced, he spent about thirty minutes with a group of boys and a couple of girls, one his own daughter. The children used all their strength jumping all over him. They laughed and giggled in their exuberant release of physical energy. He was very firm about what wrestling was all about and when they had crossed the line into play that could hurt.

The mix of children entering this play included some who had for much of the year disregarded any physical interaction with their peers. One child announced upon going home that today was the best day that he had ever had. The flushed faces and damp shirts were testament to the wisdom of making space for such play. The need for rough-and-tumble play seem to satisfy and intrigue young boys more than girls, although it comes more easily to some males than others. The fascination with all the superhero posturing and fighting spills over into many schoolrooms and dominates much playground action. We can either suppress this interest or recognize it as an expression of life.

Chapter Four

SPACES

Adventures remembered often take place in small spaces, although those places seemed so huge when one was a child. Play can happen at kitchen sinks, under the stairs, under the table draped with blankets, behind the couch, on a small patch of grass, on the sidewalk, around a tree, at the end of the waves, at the river's edge or bank, beside a puddle, in a puddle, in a gutter, near a storm drain, at the edge of the woods, in a backyard, on a stoop, under a turned over chair, on balconies and porches or in a cardboard box.

So, where did you play as a child and who was there for you? It may have been in an idyllic place or perhaps in a lane, in the midst of a downtown core, in the corridors of a tenement, in a dusty field in a small town, on the prairie or – in the case of many children in our culture – in the cul-de-sacs of suburbia. When we observe where children choose to play in public playgrounds, the space most attractive to them is often the small patch of earth under the slide structure.

We know that young children are biologically programmed to interact with their environment as investigators and explorers. The spaces in which they live and play can influence their growth towards becoming adults who are caring, flexible, tough, compassionate and industrious people.

Wading and watching.

We have "greened" the school without disrupting their play.

New patterns of raising children are emerging as more adults spend hours away from their young. People become isolated from family and community because life in the "work force" takes precedence over home or life in the immediate community. The arrangements people make for the raising of children have changed. People now are forced to cobble together numerous ways of caring for their children whether it be with a relative, a paid nanny in a home, a child care center, a preschool, school or after school care. These arrangements cover the gamut from frightening to nurturing, from sedentary and television dominated to child attentive, wholesome and respectful.

Regardless of the quality of the environment, children having to spend the majority of their days away from their kin is frightening. It is hard to imagine the stress in a young child's life of having to constantly adjust to different caregivers and places to play. In the past, there has always been something intrinsically solid about immediate kin caring for their children within the home and neighborhood. Having said this, people can change even the most inhospitable areas for children.

In Washington, D.C. where parents were afraid to let their children cross the street, gardens were created with the adults growing flowers, fruit and vegetables on the outside and children played, protected on the inside, with an area in which to dig, play with water and build forts.

In garden spaces that are wet, warm, green, growing, tree shaded, swing infested, plant covered with hills, paths, walls, seats, and sand, children feel at home.

The Evergreen Foundation in North America and Europe has volunteers working to help any school community who seeks to green playgrounds.

In the city of Roseville, California, the Tree Foundation will advise schools and home owners what trees to plant, and will also supply twenty-foot tall trees and information about how to care for them. If the task of creating gardens seems daunting, make a connection with local gardening and environmental groups. They are everywhere and ready to help.

A garden, a patch at a time.

Bev – Our priority for creating the outside area for the Roseville Community Preschool has been to provide water, pumps, sand, dirt and digging places in our yard. We have always had a little garden where we used to plant grass in boxes so children could cut it with scissors. We had a bulb garden and a few planters along with inside plants. Remembering my mother's gardens, where she grew bachelor buttons, lilacs, hollyhocks, beans, peas, and leaf lettuce, made me ache for a greener yard. Remembering the peace and the quiet and the hiding urged me on. So we, the parents and the teachers, began to create a garden, a patch at a time. The children planted seeds of which some grew and some did not, but it seemed not to matter at school. We were not ever concerned about where we planted the beans, the onions, the beets or the flowers. At some point, everything seemed to grow and the children loved to water, plant, pick, smell and even eat. One day a child was showing everyone how to suck the nectar from the honeysuckle. We created many small gardens, havens with small chairs and benches.

Children have the right to spend time in a live, green, beautiful, wild, untamed and evolving space. Each year the yard becomes

"Look out everyone, here I come!"

more verdant. About a year ago, I stepped back from the gardens and understood something really important. We had created a visually beautiful place with greened nooks and crannies but we had not interfered at all with the places to run, jump, play with water, dig in the sand and ride tricycles. We had created several small places for children where they could connect with others or seek solitude. We can see no reason for kids to be restricted with asphalt.

The parents and all the children are interested in the work at different levels; some are more passionate about it than others. I am certain, however, they will remember their time spent in the green space.

Greening the school

Bev – We water and care for the garden all summer. Justin, who had been in the school for two years, came back after summer vacation. He said to his mom in a conversation about school, "I think it's the same school but it's different. I'm pretty sure it is the same but it has more flowers and plants."

"As parents, we can take our children with us to the land. We can be with them as they climb on rocks, play in the streams and waves, dig in the rich soil of woods and garden, putter and learn. Here, on the land, we learn from each other. Here, our children's journey begins."

-- *Gary Paul Nabhan and Stephen Trimble*

"A lot of things start from seeds so small . . ."

"Play is unique. It allows the transgression of internal and external rules of life to happen; every thing has worth, it is just play. Play lets us take one step beyond reality, to play with topics and taboos that appear absolutely unchangeable, such as death, power, sex, ethics, violence, religion, justice."

- Luis Machado

Deep in the Environment

<u>Jenny</u> – In one area of the play space there is a bathtub which, for quite a long time, had been set up as a fish pond. Today, two boys were using a small plastic chair to build a trap to catch the fish. The fish, however, were smart and chose not to swim into the trap. The boys then added scoops of sand to the pond. A curious girl notice this which brought about this exchange:

Girl: *"Why are you putting mud on the fish?"*
Boy 1: *"Because we are going to kill the fish and take it home and roast it."*
Girl: *"But mud will kill the fish."*
Boy 2: *"There is mud in the ocean."*

The fish were still swimming around but they had to dodge a stone and a brick dropped with care in an attempt to stun the fish. When this was unsuccessful, the children moved the brick to another water table where an additional trap was being built.

By this time, Sally, the teacher, had been co-opted by the girl who was concerned for fish safety.

Girl: *"They are going to kill the fish."*

Sally: *"What do you think about that?"*
Girl: *"I don't want them to."*
Sally: *"Then let's go tell them."*

The girl then moved back to the fish trappers.

Girl: *"It's not nice to kill the fish."*
Boy 1: *"We are going to take him home and roast him."*
Sally: *"What about the other kids in the school who love the fish?"*
Boy 2: *"Can we have the fish food?"*
Boy 1: *"We are not really going to kill the fish, just put him where no one can see him. In the muddy water table."*
Sally: *"Let's see where you are going to put him."*

The water had drained from the reserve trap pool. A few moments later, there was more conversation around the issue of to kill or not to kill the fish.

Girl: *"Why do you have to kill the fish?"*
Boy 1: *"Because they are eating the babies."*
Boy 2: *"Because they are biting each other."*
Sally: *"These fish are alive and we are not going to hurt them."*

For these children, this play episode gave them ample opportunity for coming to terms with the daily reality of life and of possible death. They were not just passing time, amused and deflected, in the manufactured play world of toys. The children were constructing many frames of knowledge as they became involved in an intense dialogue during which they questioned values (social frame); constructed traps, dug mud and planned the trap (intellectual and physical frame); and stated how they felt about the fish, expressing both negative and positive feelings (emotional frame). Finally, the ethical frame was constructed when they took on the roles of trapper and fish hunter, counterbalanced by those of protector and guardian of the fish.

The real world is riddled with tensions between the forces of good and evil and all the shades of gray, which hover in between. Watching these children grapple with their real world once again confirmed my beliefs that play is the main conduit to learning in all areas of development socially, emotionally, physically, intellectually and spiritually.

The children, in the final stage of the play sequence described above, put the fish in a holding tub with the pondweed and refilled the cleaned pond with fresh water. Many hands helped, including the trappers, and finally the fish were lifted carefully by a child and returned to their bathtub home.

The teacher's final statement, *"These fish are alive and we are not going to hurt them,"* is an illustration of how a teacher patiently observes and enters the play to prevent the children from exercising an unacceptable action.

On the same day, in the corner of the mechanical room the children began the construction of a house made with drapes. The girl players were scurrying back and forth carrying paper, scissors, crayons and tape. Adults heard the dialogue within the walls only faintly but it was obviously riveting because the group sat there for about half an hour engrossed in conversation.

The results of longitudinal studies of children given the opportunity to play unfettered by inappropriate instruction and adult demands suggest that we should not underestimate the power of play. Yet the value of a child's self-driven play may be unappreciated by many adults. Children who have been given the opportunity to play early in their lives will often look at work tasks as a challenges that are on the same plane as play. They live their lives with a similar commitment and intensity as can be seen in young children still steeped in wonder and curiosity.

There is something profound about play, yet the full story of play has not been told. Most of us do not spend much time pondering the subject of play, or consider it as basic as, say, oxygen or sleep.

Be seriously deprived of play in childhood, though, and the consequences are likely to be dire, though delayed.

My studies of violent anti-social men (murderers, drunken drivers) revealed major play deprivation.

- Stuart L. Brown, MD from the article, Play -- Evolutionary, Essential & Universal

*Every young child has a sense
of the sacred and of ritual.*

Why do I have to live my whole life like this, people dying before me. My Aunt Connie died; she was my grandma's sister.

Stacy

*A child's story dictated to to a teacher
at the Roseville Community Preschool.*

Death of a bird

<u>Bev</u> – The children found a bird lying on the ground and with exquisite gentleness they picked it up and looked to see if it was dead. Every young child has a sense of the sacred and of ritual. They set about digging a grave and burying the bird. A celebration followed the burial. A fence to protect the sight was constructed with small wooden blocks, meticulously placed and taped together to form a circular structure. Flowers were placed on the surface of the burial sight.

Adults need to practice restraint at these times, allowing children the privilege of interpreting life and death. We can certainly watch and observe but should not intrude. Adults need not ask probing questions especially when we do not even know the answers.

"I love things like this."

<u>Bev</u> – Tom Hunter, a minstrel and educator, told me a story of a mother who had collected discarded Christmas trees in late December. She placed them in her backyard so her children could play in a forest! I love things like this and could not wait to try it at school.

Before the winter holiday, I asked the families to bring their trees to school after they were through with them. The day before the holiday break was over my co-teacher and I started digging holes in the yard deep enough for five gallon buckets. We trimmed the bottom branches of the trees, stuck the trees in the buckets, filled the buckets with sand, planted the buckets in the holes and patted sand around the tops of the buckets so you could not see them. After planting about fifteen to twenty trees we had a forest. Every tree was different: cedars, Douglas fir, Monterey pine and spruce. It was so beautiful.

The first year I started this was one of the wettest years Northern California had ever had and it rained the entire time we worked. But when the children came on Monday morning the wonder in their eyes brought tears to mine. They played and played in the forest. One minute they were bears and then the next raccoons or campers. They played hide and go seek and they chased each other. There wasn't a child who didn't play in the forest. Because it was cold and wet the forest lasted for two and a half months. One child in our school dictated a five-page list of things we would need and things he could do in the forest. Here is an excerpt from his list:

. . . hide baby stuff in the forest, in case kids have babies. Maybe a pocket knife, a fake one cause they might cut themselves with a real one. Fake tools: hammer, screwdrivers, drill and other stuff. Get them their own wallets, pens, belts, phone book, calendar, flashlight, picture book and warm pajamas. Get them suckers and slippers; wrap it up as presents. Get a razor without a blade and shaving cream. More wooden dolls, we could paint them and wrap them up. My Dad could make mail boxes; your husband could get the stuff my Dad needs. And their own warm pajamas. And my Mom could make blankets. She made me one when I was born. And we could dig a ditch through the trees and float boats.

-- Galen

Children need experiences to attach words to. The forest play was the background for this extensive list showing a young child's capacity to imagine some of the necessities for his survival. This year, with the help of many parents, we did a fifty-tree forest and two of the fathers brought a truckload of snow and tossed it over the trees for an authentic snow experience.

Frequently, parents and teachers resort to "cute" projects involving cotton balls and Styrofoam pieces to represent snow. Children are wiser than that. Cotton balls and Styrofoam pieces are just that – not snow. Certainly, you can throw it around if you like but don't call it snow.

There have to be places that belong only to children, not that adults couldn't be there if they wanted. The places I am thinking about most adults would bypass or not fit into. Children need a place of retreat, to whisper and to nest.

"Let's hide!"

There are green places in our yard, which invite a child, and maybe a friend or two, to play. There are fixed structures connected to trees and freestanding wooden climbers. Nearly everyday children tape old sheets or blankets to make hiding places in one of the structures. They drag in books, pillows, blankets, dolls, dress-up clothes, cooking utensils, leaves, flower petals and seeds to play with. Sometimes friends are invited in and sometimes it is a solitary hide away. Often, a drama is played out, complete with mothers, fathers, babies, a hospital, dogs, doctors and the jungle. The props are simple and symbolic and the flow of the story changes constantly. The designs change with the wind.

The builder said, *"Just go really slow and if you are really scared I will hold your hand."* I had the biggest lump in my throat. In this place where standing close is not intrusive or controlling but supportive, children often exhibit similar behavior.

The children ride lickety-split on the bicycle trail. All of the adults are directed to step aside and let them pass. Modeling this important behavior, I stand near children as the biker hurtles towards us, and I say quietly, *"Here comes Peter. Step off the path,"* avoiding a crash and fostering a growing awareness of themselves in space.

Standing close

Bev – *"Hey, what is this wood for?"* a child asked spotting some two-by-fours tucked away for a building project. We just kind of shrugged and acted like we didn't have any idea. So he, with great difficulty and persistence, dragged the two-by-fours halfway across the yard. He placed one end on the retaining wall and the other on the stairs leading to the tree house. He garnered the duct tape and taped the boards together. Ah, yes, he had a bridge stretched across the bicycle path. The bicyclers had to rethink their route. Then, he invited children to walk the plank. The plank was about two feet off the ground. That doesn't sound high to an adult but must have seemed really high to a child.

The child who built the bridge was standing very close as the invited guests tried to walk across. Very dramatically one lad said, *"Oh, I don't think I can do it. I might fall."*

My lounge house
Where quiet as a mouse
I stayed safe and warm
Outside raged the storm
Carpeted with soft green grass
Many gentle hours slid past
Safe and on my own
I never felt alone
Blankets draped awry
On the world I could spy
Often falling sleep
These memories I keep

Poem by a workshop participant
Whistler, B.C.

Adults who fear for their safety often restrict children. No one intends that hazards, unseen by children, should be present in their play space. But assessing potential danger and measuring risk are part of the maturing process. Risks overcome build confidence.

The cloth over the table and the cobbled together tree fort used to be the retreat spaces of childhood. Many days in the school the heavy-duty staple gun is in constant use as children initiate the carving up of the play space into individual dens. It takes little to convert a big piece of cardboard in to a play fort. Sheets and blankets can be stapled to any surface wherever a child needs to create a nest. With hula-hoops, sheer curtains and a little time, we created intimate spaces that were hung from swivel hooks both inside and outside the school.

Everyone needs a space to call their own.

"I can see you – can you see me?"

Most of children's learning is bound up in the vital action of play and playfulness.

Chapter Five

PLAY STATEMENT

The power of play sustains human beings throughout life. We must, therefore, devote attention to what fosters play in early childhood before it is too late. Spaces for play, whether in neighborhoods, homes, preschools, child care places, apartments, grandparents' homes, schools, streets, parks or playgrounds, the inside and the outside of the world children inhabit need to undergo a renaissance. Pressure from parents and policy makers calling for increasing early academic achievement has become the thrust in too many programs for young children birth through six years of age.

Children must play in multi-layered inside and outside settings, which allow every child to use materials and play space according to their own level of play. By multi-layered we mean that a simple childhood plaything such as blocks can be used both inside and outside. They take on many different facets as a play tool. Blocks in a sandbox or in a huge outdoor sand pile can be sifted over, buried and stacked by a toddler and can be used inside to build structures, bridges and roadways by four- and five-year-olds.

Most of children's learning is bound up in the vital actions of play and playfulness. If we trust children to seek out the places and spaces in which this happens naturally, we will find them learning in many places, such as when they stand at the sink dabbling in water, or maybe out in the park as they collect and mathematically line up sticks and stones. They will be learning as they are digging, scraping, poking and tunneling in any available patch of earth.

Small sticks into triangles

Jenny - I watched a small boy in the yard of his dusty Pakistani hut encampment spend at least two hours busily assembling a handful of small sticks into rectangles. He used small lengths of cassette tape to tie the sticks together. His dexterity and concentration was remarkable. In a school down the street small, children in uniform were sitting at tables filling in ditto sheets of arithmetic sums. I could not help but wonder who was learning to be a real problem solver.

The primal need to play, repeating actions each and every day, is the grist of childhood. All too quickly we, as adults, put the lid on such exuberance and endeavor. In the name of schooling and preparing young children for the future, we often derail them from the process of leaping, tumbling, murmuring, talking and laughing. All of this is essential in their learning and growing.

Look around and watch for child-driven play constructions. Learn to recognize their value in terms of learning the basic concepts such as mathematics, physics, architecture, engineering and spatial intelligence. They are all around us in the form of skateboard ramps, hopscotch patterns, rope swings in trees, impromptu tents and most things home-made with scrounged materials.

We need to combine our understanding of what is important for play with our energy, dollars, rubles, pounds or Euro dollars so that we build space where children can gather and find their own forest, pool, stream, walls, mounds, huts and pathways. Thus we need to give children time to work each day at reshaping the terrain and infusing their minds and bodies with the joy of play.

In our work with children it helps to be aware of the connections between children's play and the occupations,

The primal need to play, repeating actions each and every day, is the grist of childhood.

"Play is probably the most obvious real world situation which coerces learners into using language."

- Brian Cambourne

. . . infusing their minds and bodies with the joy of play.

fields of expertise or disciplines that exist in the larger world. In doing so, we will be less likely to interfere, interrupt or direct their play.

The list of play occupations does not intend to suggest that children at play will take on the following adult roles. But they may help to reveal the complicated and important task of becoming an astute play observer. We know that the time spent playing during childhood strengthens a person in all areas of human endeavor. Regardless of our age when we encounter new experiences in life, if we have the capacity to play, then we learn and grow.

Below is a partial list of some of these "play occupations" and perhaps you will add your own observations as you hang around with kids.

The block builder or woodworker may carry the seed of an architect, a carpenter, engineer, interior designer, fence builder or mathematician.

The grinders, mixers and diggers may become the bakers, landscape architects, gardeners, farmers and chemists.

The dramatic players may evolve into politicians, actors, newspaper reporters, teachers, space travelers, explorers or nurses as well as becoming mothers, fathers, grandfathers and grandmothers, aunts, uncles and cousins.

The natural explorers who enjoy the bugs and the beasts may develop into the environmental scientists, the anthropologists, veterinarians, birdwatchers, undertakers or meteorologists.

Off to the market.

The tappers and bangers may eventually be musicians, mechanics, composers, lighting experts, computer programmers or plumbers.

During play, a variety of roles will emerge, some of which can be best suited to the adult play partner. The following story demonstrates how adults need to take their cues from the children.

"Just the piece I need."

<u>Bev</u> – My grandson Zac often wants me to play Duplos ™. What I do is sit with a huge box of the pieces on my lap, rummage through and find unusual pieces and hand them to him saying, *"Look at this piece."* Sometimes he rejects the piece with a look of disdain but, often, he grins and says, *"Just the piece I need."* I am the follower, not the LEADER, in this undertaking.

This play is richer if adults and older children, who have not lost their capacity to play, enter into the play to support, encourage, supply play props and to once in a while act as play partners.

The skills of the adult play partners are obvious when they are able to rein in their own ego and let the child direct, restructure and reorganize the materials and the direction of the play.

Polar bear plunge

<u>Jenny</u> – Two girls decked out in the finery of princesses, complete with heeled shoes, strut confidently through the muddy, turbulent water without a backward glance as another player prepares for a "polar bear" plunge.

Sometimes, the adults' sense of propriety causes them to step in and stop the dramatic play. The children in

"My shoes are ruined!"

Homo sapien culture is derived from children's play. As our children are no longer playing in the natural world, the question arises . . . what is the future of our culture and will we, because of this change, be evolving to the next level for better or worse?

- B. Hughes

both cases were deeply involved in dramatic play either as princesses or as a deep-sea diver. The adult play partner provides a towel, dry clothes and hot chocolate, a small price to pay for uninhibited confidence and courage. In much of children's play you need to take the position of the fly on the wall and just watch.

Bev – What I ask myself before opening my mouth and moving in to redirect or to stop the action is, *"Will the end of the world come as a result of this play,"* or *"Could the players learn something about themselves and others?"* In the situation described above, what about the science of water, cold, depth, goose bumps and about taking care of yourself? Finally, from me, the provider of towels and hot chocolate, they learn a little about taking care of each other.

Table top -- flip the prop

Bev – In the school, there is a fold down table with two large holes so children can stand up and reach to more areas of the table. The table is called the "train table" because usually the Brio™ train is on it as it is today. Two or three children walked up and looked at the train and started to remove the track. It is obvious to me that they wanted something else on this table. Too often adults respond with, *"The train is set up; don't take it off."* I have learned to always ask myself,*"Why not?"* and then try to help in any way. Justin asked me to help him remove the train and then he spent several minutes building with blocks on the table.

We need to get back to what is important – the child's inquiring mind. The adult play partner must to be ready to act expeditiously upon a request for restructure.

Rich experiences in using all the senses, therefore, are not only essential for development but also critical for survival.

Thinkers, philosophers and teachers have expanded our understanding of the importance and value of childhood and play. Researchers have observed, documented and written extensively about intellectual and social growth rooted in play experiences. Practitioners and teachers put into practice many of the ideas about the way children grow and learn in rich adaptable environments. The echoes of the work of these thinkers and teachers have bounced back and forth and helped form the body of knowledge upon which we draw when creating environments for young children. More than ever we must stand firm against the onslaught of the demand for early academic instruction for young children.

Today we have a foundation of knowledge about play and development. Homo sapiens need a long span of time to reach maturity. The task of infancy and early childhood is to move from a dependent infant into an interdependent child. Children grow and learn with the support of caring

Stages of Play – solitary, parallel and associative.

adults who encourage them to use their senses of sound, touch, smell, taste and sight.

The sound of the human voice as it surrounds children, including songs, rhymes, chants and chatter, of the human voice, lays the foundation for speech. The babbling baby needs speaking, singing, chanting adults to support the development and refinement of language. It is within the relationship between the adults and children that spoken language can flourish.

Babies will seek to touch everything within reach. Just watch a baby repeatedly crumple a piece of paper. It's the way they learn. If they haven't touched it, moved it, taken it apart or manipulated it, it can't be in their brain.

Smell is a strong thread to memory. If children have not had the opportunity to differentiate between the scent of lavender and Pinesol™, they will have limited access to sensory pleasure and information. Similarly, playing only with plastic look-alike food robs children of the experience of change, texture, smell and taste.

The brain needs visual stimulation and children are sensitive to patterns from birth. This necessary stimulation will not occur if a child's visual experiences are limited to interior rooms that are bland, artificial and lack natural beauty. Cloud patterns and leaf movement, which inspired artists such as Claude Monet and Leonardo da Vinci, and scientists such as Albert Einstein, provide rich stimulation in the constantly changing patterns they produce in a natural way.

A factor of paramount importance in the growth and development of young children is that adults understand and respect that there are things young children cannot do. This is not because children have failed to understand the directions or expectations but because they are only concerned with the here and now, and are unable to follow spoken directions, which are often too long and complicated.

There are some words we use that are contentious such as "sharing." So often we hear an adult demanding upon request that children share their possessions. When children have had sufficient time to take possession of an object, they will probably be ready to share. We seem to think that the exercise of sharing will make our children socially acceptable in the adult world but fail to recognize that children are only able to share when they are developmentally ready to understand the concept of give-and-take.

"I don't want to share my toy, I want to show it!"

Bev – Eric brought something from home to show the other children. We do not call it sharing, understanding that children cannot do that. At the end of the morning we bring the "home stuff" box over to the rug area and say, "If you brought something to show the other children, get it out of the basket and find somebody to show it to." Eric's mother noticed several children wanting to see what Eric brought, but Eric was clutching his possession close to his chest. She asked: "Eric, why are you not showing the children what you brought?" He said, "Somebody said 'It's sharing time,' and I don't want to share my toy, I want to show it."

Adults generally think children aren't listening. Some adult must have inadvertently used the sharing word. Children must fully possess and understand ownership before they can share. Sharing is a developmental process. An adult who understands would say to the waiting child, "Ask him if you can use it when he is through." This might precipitate anguish and crying. However, if the environment has enough options for play, the child who is waiting for a turn could find something else to do. Here's a good point to remember: If the stuff is generic, like spoons, scoops, sand, bottles or bits of wood then there can be "lots," enough for everybody which cuts down the demand for ownership.

Are you wondering at what age a child will be able to share? It depends upon whether the child has gone through the egocentric stage first. It is during the egocentric stage of life that children must not be put under pressure to share. Forcing children to share too early is detrimental because it does not help them to become less self-centered and empathetic to other people's needs. Instead, it may make children overly possessive, resistant and fearful.

The "Egg"-pire State Building

A playful encounter with the world does not supply the right or wrong answers to problems -- but it expands the avenues for finding solutions.

Misguided efforts to impose rules

<u>Jenny</u> – The following accident did not take place at Roseville Community Preschool but is outlined here to illustrate how often adults are misguided in their efforts to impose rules for safety.

A small boy wearing a jacket is swinging on a swing. The rule is that you must give up the swing if you get off. After swinging a while and becoming hot, the boy attempts to circumvent the rule and takes both hands off the swing ropes (while still in motion) to remove his jacket, falls to the ground and fractures his arms.

This unfortunate accident shows that adults in setting the rules for the use of the swing had failed to understand that a child who is egocentric will only be able to interpret the rule literally and be unable to realize that the swing was his until he had had enough swinging.

By speeding up the process of children joining the adult world we may satisfy our need for a child to fit in and to be liked. But if expectations of children during their egocentric stage are too high the result may be that we are left with more, not fewer, adults who are unable to take care of themselves and of others.

And by the way, young children cannot take turns. They can be *made* to take turns, but once the controls are off their behavior reverts to the egocentric. Sharing and taking turns develop in a natural way only when children have had the opportunity to use, to have, to possess a toy until their need to play with it has been satisfied.

Sometimes a child will put the plaything down and another child will begin to play with it. The first child will begin to cry and want the toy returned. Here is the developmental opportunity; "He has it now, ask him if you can use it when he's done." Or, for the preverbal child, it is enough to say, "When he's done."

Children are very present and collect information *only if it is important to them*. In other words, expecting children to remember a set of rules, that are completely meaningless and incomprehensible, is fruitless. If this weren't the case, no parent would ever be heard saying, "How many times have I told you?" or "Remember what I said?"

Here is a story we have heard from more than one family:

In an effort to prepare their young son for the possibility of an unexpected encounter with a stranger, a mother spent one month drilling the child on what to do. At the end of that time she decided to test him by asking, "Suppose a man comes up to you and says, 'Little boy, would you like some candy?' What are you going to say?" The boy replied, "Trick or treat?" The only word a young child would hear in that exchange is, CANDY.

If I could give a gift to parents it would be to give them the ability to watch and to trust the child, to enjoy them. For example, *not sharing* is productive in this way; if the child is immersed in not sharing, once they complete that stage, they are much more likely to become generous adults.

Children cannot be forced to cooperate with each other until they have reached the stage of maturity when it becomes possible. The environment, however, can be set up to encourage such interaction.

Waiting for the big one.

"I think I'll grow me a dinosaur."

"I think children are safe here from being "encouraged" (prodded, coaxed) to act out the delight adults want them to experience. They get to choose, or not, for themselves what they shall enter into. Sometimes I observed things for a long time then decided to try them -- or not. Once an adult had prodded me (prodded as distinct from simply and quietly articulating the opportunity), it was no longer the same experience of choosing the world for myself."

- Barry Bussewitz

Play Stages

Solitary • Parallel • Onlooker • Associative • Cooperative

What follows is a simple outline of the play stages.

Babies and toddlers as **SOLITARY** players focus upon every stimulus that surrounds them. A baby confronted with any object on the floor will edge towards it with the tenacity of a long-distance runner. She will not be deflected from her endeavor. She will grab the object and proceed to take it apart and to explore its properties. She plays alone, hence the term solitary.

From toddler hood on, with enough materials available, the inquisitive young child plays **PARALLEL** to other children often without realizing others have entered their space.

Sometimes a child may seem perfectly satisfied just to watch others paint, dig, pour, dance and sing. This **ONLOOKER** stage is one adults have a hard time respecting. The tendency is to cajole, encourage (or pester) the child into participating rather than allowing them to observe from the periphery.

ASSOCIATIVE players in a preschool may clamber onto the back of a tricycle for a ride with another child that goes nowhere. They engage in the same activity as others but without much interaction.

When children cluster around the water hole and dig for hours, working together to solve the problems of escaping water, they have moved to the **COOPERATIVE** stage. Here they are actively engaging with others to reach a common play goal.

Too often, children are asked to work at the cooperative stage without consideration for all the other stages.

Children cannot be forced to cooperate with each other until they have reached the stage of maturity when it becomes possible. The environment, however, can be set up to encourage such interaction.

All people, young and old, spend part of each day in each stage. For instance, the reaper standing in the midst of the garden is an example of solitary play behavior.

The adults sitting side by side on a park bench, seeking contact without any long-term interactions are demonstrating parallel play.

People crammed on benches cheering for their favorite sport's team are onlookers.

Someone leaving the car in the garage and taking the bus, sitting with others en route to work is typical of associative behavior.

Parents meeting to reconstruct the school play yard, modifying, discussing and reworking their ideas to develop a workable plan, are demonstrating the cooperative stage. If the stages of play are not fully understood, acknowledged and internalized then adults often ask children to involve themselves with materials and with other children without understanding their capacity and readiness to respond. Children who are not at the cooperative stage expected to share and take turns have no comprehension of why they need to do this. They may be coerced into compliance but they may never truly become fully cooperative and empathetic adults, able to submerge their own egocentric needs for the good of another person or group.

We must understand the natural progression of development it cannot be hurried and moreover, it has it's own timetable. If you understand and support the process, most humans will become competent, functioning adults.

Cooperative Play . . . actively engaging with others to reach a common play goal.

Play is the energy and passion that drives the explorer, that jangles the composer, that captures the anthropologist, that anchors the architect, that animates the artist, that hammers the carpenter, that inspires the author, that motivates the teacher, that stirs the designer, that goads the negotiator and ferrets out the gardener. In short, play is the very pulse of life.

The baby, as its brain registers experiences, gains impressions of the object, its texture, its taste and its sound. Throughout infancy and into childhood children play with the objects and materials that pepper the spaces and places they inhabit. Deprivation starts early if a child has limited and sterile spaces in which to spend time. Environments that are rich, diverse and enticing with many accessible objects and "stuff" are essential for providing memory hooks for the baby.

It is important that every home has a cupboard at child height filled with old pots, pans, wooden spoons, spatulas and lids for banging, smacking and stirring. The child explores, bangs and taps these props and later uses them symbolically, perhaps as a drum or as a pretend cooking utensil.

Over and over and over

Bev – As a young child, my granddaughter Meghan literally spent hours washing dishes. Anytime I would drop by to say hello there she would be washing the plastic dishes and the pots and pans over and over and over. Children often repeat and revisit play processes such as this much to the bewilderment of adults who tend to view them as detours in children's orderly and linear mastery of skills. Small tables or an overturned box can be placed somewhere in the yard where the child can find water, dirt and sand to make and bake mud pies. Flour could be added, so could salt. Food coloring is the frosting on the cake. The most lasting memories for a child is mud pie play.

Stones in the gutter

Jenny – Three small children waiting to see their dad run past in a marathon event are easily engaged. While they wait, they become interested in a small pile of stones in the gutter, which immediately become the play objects.

They play by constantly reforming and reconstructing patterns, which have meaning for them. Their play is a self-chosen and self-directed activity.

Children playing in a heap of sand with buckets of water on hand are attempting to build and rebuild their sandscapes. They are developing brain connections, which will serve as intellectual pathways for future problem solving.

Adults meeting a computer for the first time can master it more easily if they are comfortable enough to play about with the technology and are not terrified of making mistakes.

It is our opinion that people stay fully alive when play has been part of both their young life as well as their adult years. Their play experiences equip them with curiosity and a willing involvement in the world around them that helps them come to terms with the unknown and to delight in the present. They are inspired and alive.

A playful encounter with the world does not supply the right or wrong answers to problems but it expands the avenues for finding solutions. Players can look outside the box or known body of knowledge to find possible solutions to the myriad problems, which haunt and challenge every generation of people who inhabit this fragile and fascinating space called planet Earth.

You walk the path of childhood only once in life. It is a whisper in time and yet the ramifications of narrowing the possibilities for play leave us with many hollow people cut adrift in a wasteland. At the beginning of the twenty-first century our society often seems like a wasteland; a wasteland of dissatisfaction, of unfulfilled dreams, of depleted souls, of brash commercialism. We live in a culture that concentrates far too much on the acquisition of material wealth, which for many people, is devoid of any true fulfillment. What and who will sustain our children? We believe that play is unmatched in its power to sustain children throughout their entire lives. The people who can make a difference in the lives of children are the friends, fathers, mothers, aunts, uncles, grandparents, guides, play partners, teachers and elders that surround them. Many children come from fragmented families and communities in disarray. We must all take part in the care of children through our nurturing and our understanding of the importance of their need to play.

"Play is the highest expression of human development in childhood, for it alone is the free expression of what is in a child's soul."

- Fredrick Froebel

Chapter Six

ART

"Yes, but my heart wasn't finished!"

The early art of cave painting, petroglyphs and pictographs communicated from one generation to the next the story of that time and place.

"If we hope for our children that they will become full human beings and that they will move towards actualizing the potentialities that they have, then, as nearly as I can make out, the only kind of education in existence today that has any faint inkling of such goals is art education."

- Abraham Maslow

We believe Maslow was referring to something other than twenty-five identical rainbows, jack-o'-lanterns, turkeys, pilgrim hats, snowmen, or any theme-based color-by-number art. Art is visionary. Art propels us into realms beyond our reality. Children react to and build upon the visual stimulus of their first few scribbles on the paper. As time goes on, this process involves the combination of lines and circles and forms, markings and shapes. This is a developmental process and when respected, it allows the individual to take pleasure in expressing themselves through the arts. When we ignore the process, the satisfaction that art can provide the artist is usurped for the benefit of pleasing others. Children today must be provided with the opportunity to embrace this process, to use paper, paint, string, glue, glitter, tape, ribbon, and whatever else they can use, to further their understanding of their world.

Our responsibility is to provide an extensive variety of tools and materials so that children can experiment and become comfortable with expressing themselves. Children involved in art are completely present and their art is

Young children who have not been coerced or intimidated by demands which throttle their natural exuberance and involvement with art have, we believe, a clearer path to becoming creative problem solvers and thinkers.

"Who needs paper?"

always process-oriented and rarely about the final product unless adults make that the priority.

Art for a child or for an adult is not a once a week "We do art on Friday afternoon" activity, but an ongoing response to the way in which we see things and feel things in our lives.

Recall the last time, as an adult; you stood before a work of art. Remember feeling moved beyond being able to say how you felt without verbally stumbling? There were no words to describe the feelings, the depth of emotion and the extent to which you were affected by the work. Some people may faint at the sight of Michelangelo's *David*. Can we be sure that children are not experiencing their art on a level that for them is just as deep? Few of us introduce ourselves to another adult as *an artist* yet nonetheless, we often feel qualified to critique or intrude into children's art. Just as art is an individual expression, so too is the interpretation of the viewer. Art makes us think. When we write words on a child's piece of art, we limit everyone else's opportunity to personalize the experience. The art becomes the words. We doubt if Picasso would have been able to control himself if someone had said, "Oh how nice, you have just split the human face into two parts. I see some unusual lines here."

Art is beyond the realm of known language. It lies beneath the skin of language. In other words, there are no words to describe the feelings, the emotions, the pleasure, the pain or the reasons for painting, scribbling and daubing. Through art, humans actualize and internalize experience. When adults attempt to interpret a child's art or asks the child, *"tell me about your picture,"* they diminish the value of the art experience. Rather than leave the experience in the realm of the majestic, art becomes mundane.

Young children who have not been coerced or intimidated by demands, which throttle their natural exuberance and involvement with art, have a clearer path to becoming creative problem solvers and thinkers. Art for young children, apart from being enthralling, influences problem solving.

There is a time for expanding the world of art for children with the help of docents, artists, craftsmen and such, but we need to take care we do not get things out of order. Refinement and technique must wait their turn.

At a conference twice a year in Roseville, California, about one hundred adults gather in a large room with many tables and spaces that are set up for undirected, self-driven art play. There are no standards or expectations put upon the art players, they just immerse themselves in the glories of massive quantities of quality paint, paper, glue, chalk, crayon, clay and implements rarely found in the traditional classroom.

The volume and diversity of artwork is stunning but the true value is the massaging of the spirit and soul, which appears to take place. The art experience is the thread of connection taken back by participants to communities where art is rightfully placed at the hub of creative experience.

"I love art, Bev Bos."

<u>Bev</u> – I observed Stephen, an eight-year-old, who came to the summer program and ran frantically from one art

"In art you are either a revolutionary or a plagiarist."

- Paul Gauguin

activity to another (we offer five to six different creative art activities everyday during summer school). The perspiration was just dripping off his nose. I stood close to him and I think he sensed my interest in what he was doing. He turned to me and said, *"I love art, Bev Bos, and I never get a chance to do all the art I want to do, so I have to do lots of it while I am here."*

The best thing parents can do is to have a variety of art materials at home. Cover the kitchen table with paper and let everyone scribble and doodle. This is not a competition or display, but just pure play and enjoyment.

Seventeen pictures in one day.

Bev – A four-year-old child in the school painted seventeen pictures in one day. Her mother very quietly said to me, *"I don't think she will ever be in another place where she will be allowed to paint seventeen pictures in one day."*

We did not comment on the art, we were just the suppliers, keeping the paint and the paper coming.

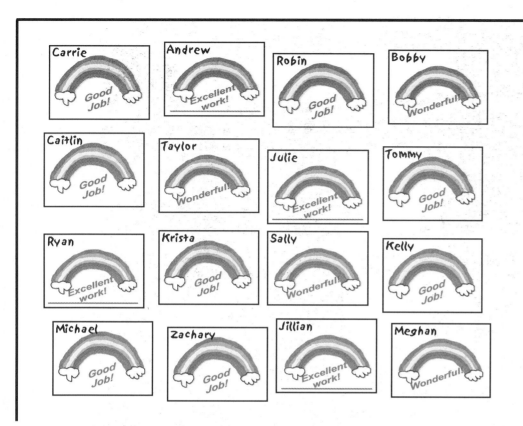

We crush children's creative spirit by grading art and by comparing one child's art to another's. If we want children to persist with art, we must avoid any form of comparison.

"But I only got to paint one."

<u>Bev</u> – A mother of a child who used to be in the preschool program told me this story about her child. She picked him up at kindergarten and he seemed a bit melancholy. She tried to lighten his sadness and remarked, *"You did get to paint today."*

He responded, *"But I only got to paint one."*
She said, *"You did get to paint, though."*
He said, *"Yes, but my heart wasn't finished."*

"We will make room."

<u>Bev</u> – One day I removed the legs from the Plexiglas easel and duct taped it between two tables. I put paper on top and magnetic marbles dipped in paint with magnetic paddles underneath with which to move the marbles around on the paper. The enthusiasm of the children was overwhelming. My response was, *"Quick, get another easel and take the legs off it."* One of the adults responded, *"We don't have room for another easel."* To which I replied, *"We can make room."*

Providing the very best kind of art program for young children takes more than a plan, more than curriculum, more than another new idea, more than buying another gizmo. It can only happen when the adults ask the same question of themselves that they ask of children: *"What would happen if . . .?"*

When children are captivated by an activity and obviously need more time, space and material to wallow in it, and other children are interested, we need to move as quickly as possible to change the physical environment. When changes in the environment need to happen the adults must do the adjusting. If we believe in the worth of immersion in play, then we must adjust our plan to meet the needs of the child. Two things you can change: your plan and your materials. You cannot change the needs of the child.

Just for a moment, think of the places our ancestors have left their records of life. They used flat surfaces, walls of the cave, the flat of a stone, skins of animals, canvas, wood, parchment, and they learned to use the natural pigments to prepare paint. If we provide good quality paint, masses of paper, glue and clay and make them easily available to children, we will provide them with the materials to begin artistic expression.

Furthermore, we can enrich the process for children by providing a wider variety of tools. Even for those who may not consider themselves artists have noticed that many artists have pushed the parameters of artistic expression by playing with unusual materials and tools. It is important that teachers and parents are consistent and thoughtful in

Untitled.

the way they organize art activities for young children.

Creativity and structure can exist side by side. In other words, the space you have available for art needs to be organized in the best possible way. Well-organized containers, extra materials, and an art cart, organized basket or boxes can be useful. At home, covering tables with heavy plastic taped securely underneath eases cleaning up. Children need to know where to find things so they can do art on a whim.

Children, also, push the parameters of artistic expression, especially when they are first introduced to the materials. For instance, they may often use what *looks* like too much paint or glitter. But what is it really? It is not misbehavior, it is experimentation. When adults do not provide sufficient time, materials and space they crush the artistic spirit.

Over the past thirty-five years we have collected hundreds of things to paint with. It helps to step away from the traditional supply sources of art materials. Visit the hardware store and ask yourself, *"Could the children paint with this?"* (see p. 88) Opportunities abound for discovering unconventional paint utensils in many places.

Collages have a random quality, which make them an attractive art form for children. The collage material can be easily and thoughtfully organized in trays on a work table so that children can gather their own tray and proceed to another work table to create collage art.

At one time the collages we did followed the seasons, holidays or color themes. We don't do that anymore. Art is a much more important experience than putting red pieces of paper on a white background to make a valentine picture. Stop trying to determine such outcomes and leave the red paper, doilies, red feathers and glitter to be used anytime. We have as wide a range of scraps, snippets, threads, cloths and paper of as many lengths and textures as we can scrounge and we keep the supply coming. The children are free to experiment, change, invent and create with whatever materials are available. The children's requests for different materials are also honored.

The adult role in children's art is to provide the materials and space and then to stand back and let the children use materials as they seem fit. Most of the adult energy is better employed in setting up the art space and helping with clean up. Once the artists are at play with the materials then the adult role is quiet support.

Sometimes I quietly hang around in case a child needs to talk to me. I pay attention to the child, not to my own need to understand the art or what the child has in mind. The adult must never, in our opinion, present an image or model that the children are expected to copy or reproduce. And for an adult to suggest some blue or red paint would make a difference is unnecessary. This seems to happen more often with holiday art than at other times. In our fervor over celebrations we require children to make identical Easter bunnies, jack-o'-lanterns and Santa Clauses. It is insulting because it removes from the children the opportunity to create their own images. To create means to bring something into existence. What happens early in the child's life is the suppression of the child's inherent creative ability by the setting of adult standards. This happens when models are presented or theme-directed art is insisted upon.

"It is not what the child does with the materials but what the materials do to the child."
- Marilyn Campbell

"Just one final touch-up."

We can also crush children's creative spirit by grading art and by comparing one child's art to another's. If we want children to persist with art, we must avoid any form of comparison. Evaluating one child's art by saying, *"Oh, that's beautiful,"* or, *"Oh, how wonderful,"* or, *"You made wavy lines,"* undermines the child's ownership of the art experience. Praising art interferes with the child/artist's opportunity to reflect on what they have done and makes the child dependent upon the adult's response to know if their art is valid. Another danger is that other children, who may not be seeking your approval, could feel less secure with their own accomplishment. Evaluation is detrimental to growth. And what if you don't say something the next time? Does the child infer that the work is not wonderful this time? Children do art for art's sake, to satisfy a need inside, to nurture the creative self. Art stands on its own.

What we all need to do is immerse ourselves in all forms of art with the hope that we can rediscover our own indwelling art spirit.

Every child is an artist. The problem is how to remain an artist once he grows up.

- Pablo Picasso

easels

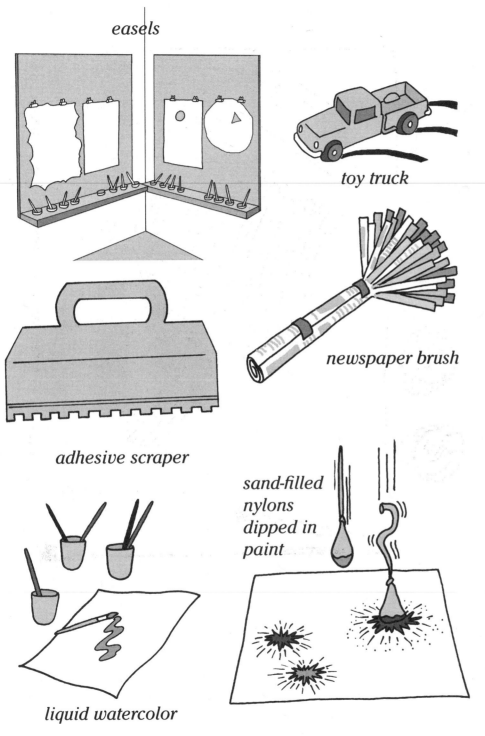

toy truck

newspaper brush

adhesive scraper

liquid watercolor

sand-filled nylons dipped in paint

What we want this part of the book to be is the start of the art experience for you and your children. What we imagine as we write this book is that some of you may have had limited art experiences in your life, with no opportunity to paint or color without being critiqued or compared to others. We imagine it might be like a whole kitchen full of food without any idea about proportions, flavours or how things might blend or compliment each other. What follows are some of the things we provide young children with to give them the chance to make the most of their art experience.

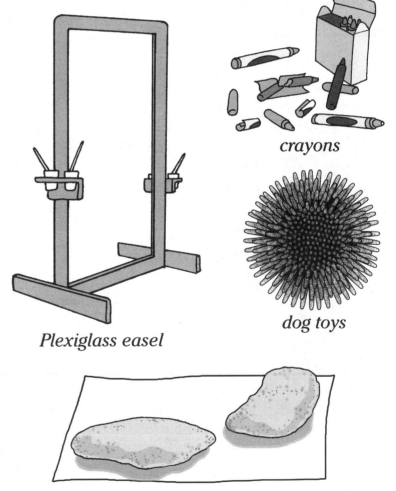

crayons

dog toys

Plexiglass easel

natural sponges

Art Supply List

This list is a good place to start your art studio.

Good quality paper
Brayers
Spray bottles
Sponges - especially natural ones
Scrapers
Tile adhesive scrapers
Shaving brushes
Body massage rollers
Carved wooden table legs
Brushes - all kinds and sizes
Rubber band brushes
Squeegies
Paint rollers - large and small
Nylon sock-filled with sand
Splatter screens
Tiles
Feather dusters
Toy cars and trucks
Spools
Dog toys
Crayons
Muffin tins
Newspaper brushes
Liquid watercolor
Tempera paint
Clay
Straws
Art chalk
Sidewalk chalk

Awe and reverence.

Chapter Seven

SCIENCE

Elemental Play

"What you're looking for is whatever the hell you find!"
- Richard Feynman

The sense of wonder, curiosity, inquiry, energy and eagerness to pursue the why and what of everything is what makes young children scientists. With curious parents and teachers exploring along with the children, science becomes "the pleasure of finding things out."

Science is not learned from a book; it must be hands-on. Science is elemental play. Elemental play, in this context, is the play, which takes place with the four basic elements of earth, water, air and fire. There are obviously some constraints with certain aspects of "elemental play" with very young children, but apart from fire the other three are everywhere.

We have seen the proliferation of environmental programs for children that concentrate on saving plants, animals and birds and attempting to protect ecosystems around the world. This dissemination of information regarding global environmental issues can detract from young children's need to make sense of and to understand the immediate. Their world is local. The gutter outside the schoolyard, the weeds in the sidewalk cracks and the dribble of the struggling local stream are the habitats most easily accessible to young children.

In every area of the school science is happening. Science is happening when children are playing with natural materials or digging in the sand or

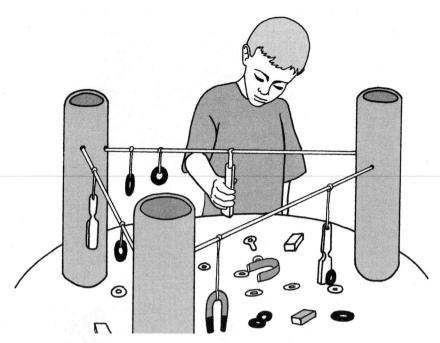

*"Too much information
can swamp the boat of wonder."*
- Chet Raymo

garden. Science is also making things bubble over again and again. When we are doing art we experience volume, light, color, shadow, motion and wetness. Consider sound, vibration and timbre when we play around with music. Blocks provide us with many math, engineering and design experiences.

The school or home garden – with its constant changes and cycles, the compost piles, the worms and bugs and the sowing and harvesting – provides the greatest opportunity for children to connect and observe change.

Magnets are another way children can interact with their immediate world. Playing with magnets often mesmerizes children and adults alike. There is a deep desire to under-

stand the force of magnetism. Unlike electricity, which we cannot so readily experiment with, magnets can move objects through space and give one a sense of power.

"Carpet tubes + metal rods = magnet table."

<u>Bev</u> – Noticing the profound interest in magnets I decided to give more time, space and thought to magnets. On the top of a table I taped three carpet tubes upright (see illustration) and connected the tubes with metal rods. I hung magnetic paddles at different heights from the metal rods. On the table I put nuts, bolts, paper clips, spoons, forks, washers, nails and smaller magnets. I also included many objects that were not magnetic. The children made the hanging magnets spin and move. Later they got under the table and made the objects on top of the table spin and jump by hold magnets against the bottom of the table.

"I don't think magnets work in water."

<u>Bev</u> – One morning a child came dashing in and said to me, "Bev Bos, I don't think magnets work in water." I said, "We must find out."

We got a pan of water and some blocks of wood to raise the pan in case he wanted to try magnets under the pan. He arranged the pan below one of the metal rods and started to play. He put small magnets in the water and then used a magnetic paddle under the pan to test his hypothesis. When he saw the results, he said with awe in his voice, *"I was wrong."* He asked if we had aluminum foil and I quickly provided a roll. He made boats and tried to move them with the paddle. He said, *"Ah, they are not moving."* I just watched. He surveyed the supplies and finally selected some small ring magnets and put them gently in the boats. He was then able to move them with the magnetic paddles.

Here a child begins to construct his own knowledge through play rather than from interacting with a commercially produced toy. The adult role here was to establish a basic magnetic play environment and then respond to the child's curiosity. I didn't ask, but my hunch was that this child had thought about water and magnets for quite a long time, perhaps from the moment he left the magnetic table the day before.

"I think we got it all."

<u>Bev</u> – On an incredibly windy day I grabbed a thirty gallon black plastic bag and I bolted through the school. A child asked, *"What are YOU going to do?"*

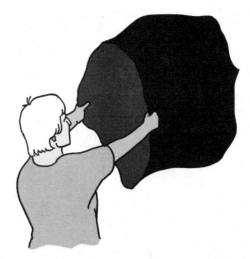

"I'm going to get a bag of air!"

"I am going to get a bag of air," I replied.

Outside I held the bag high over my head and it filled to a glorious proportion. I quickly closed the top of the bag with a twist tie and proclaimed, *"I have a bag of air."*

All the children screamed, *"I need a bag of air, too."*

All of the children got bags and let the wind fill them. Some of them attached pieces of string to the top and ran with huge bags of wind behind them. The wind swooped away one of the bags from a child and she cried, *"My air! My air! My bag of air!"* We had to go outside the fence to retrieve her bag of air. A short time later, just for a moment the wind stopped blowing.

A child whispered, *"I think we got it all."*

Some of the children sat on the bags. At the end of the day all of the children took their bags of air home.

Science cannot be restricted to *"the prepared for"* experiment. The usual science class model of introducing

Beware the science activity book which calls the chemical reaction between vinegar and baking soda a "volcano."

Inaccurate information confuses children, as well as adults, and it tends to stop any further inquiry.

new terms and apparatus, modeling proper procedure and having the children attempt to duplicate the teacher's experiment does more to discourage scientific inquiry than encourage it. We always need to be on the lookout for a chance to play with elements such as air, water, energy and matter and then at the end of the play, perhaps much later we can give a name to the experience.

Children need to experience everything firsthand. A walk in forest, a run through the puddles, a crawl through the grass, the feel of the sun's warmth on the body, the power of the wind, the wetness of rain and the cold softness of snow should be experienced, not on a video or on the television, but out and about where they live. Certainly many traditional songs about weather and water are part of childhood but we believe young children do not always make the connection between the words of the songs and reality. Sing those songs and go outside and leave the symbolic weather chart for some other time.

There is an excitement about the weather for children that need to be actualized through experience. They experience weather by gathering the wind in a bag, collecting rain in a pan, melting ice and snow, jumping in the rain puddle and peering through the fog. Remember children must have experiences to which they can attach words.

Scientific understanding is undermined by inaccurate information and language. Beware of the science activity book which calls the chemical reaction between vinegar and baking soda a "volcano." It is an eruption but we must chose our words carefully. It would be far better to say a chemical reaction has occurred and a gas has been produced. Ask someone from Kansas if they have seen a "tornado in a jar" and they will likely laugh. The attempt here is to entice adults (parents and teachers) and children to be comfortable with scientific inquiry by making it seem cute. Science is not cute and especially not magic, but the results can sometimes *appear* magical to both adults and children. When their interest is captured they will try again to test, hypothesize, observe and replicate.

Another example of the inaccurate use of language would be filling a bottle with blue water and oil and calling it "the ocean." Again, a more accurate interpretation would be to discuss wave action which can be observed as you turn the bottle end upon end.

Scientific words, such as wave action, can be used with young children. This respects the work the children are doing in building literacy and scientific understanding. It is important to be as accurate as possible with language when working with children. Inaccurate information confuses children, as well as adults, and it tends to stop any further inquiry.

Science, by definition, is systematized knowledge derived from observation, study and experimentation carried on in order to determine the nature or principles of what is being studied.

Magic, by definition, is the general term for any of the supposed arts of producing marvelous effects by supernatural or occult power – *the opposite of science.*

Twenty pounds of flax.

Bev – Two large flat pans about eight inches deep are placed upon a low table and filled with twenty pounds of flaxseed which is mixed by an adult with very warm water. After it has cooled a little the children investigate it. They do this in numerous ways from sticking in a finger or their whole hand at the beginning. They stirred it, felt it, smelled it and ultimately stood in it up to mid calf. One child particularly enjoyed mushing around with her bare feet in the warm gooey substance.

Flax seed, warm water and child.

"This is just what I need."

This is just what I need.

<u>Bev</u> – A child came into the school and sat down with his mother and made a list of ingredients. He brought it to me and said, *"This is what I need to do my experiment: flour, soda, salt, vinegar and oil."* Bowls were brought forth and he proceeded to scoop, mix and stir. Immediately there were six other children with a list of ingredients. They were prepared to be chemists and chefs. All the concoctions the children made were baked and many of them were taken home.

This form of activity in which the children's needs were taken seriously supports children's drive to become autonomous risk takers and critical thinkers.

When I have a conversation with someone who tries out new ideas, invents new ways of doing things or who can fix just about anything, I always ask about their childhood. Without fail they talk about their parents giving them the time and the space to tinker around with things. They were provided with old bikes, telephones, radios or motors, and as they grew older, anything they could take a screwdriver or a wrench to.

Frequently in early childhood programs and in homes with young children, kinesthetic intelligence is neglected. It is important that everyone is given the opportunity to further develop manual dexterity. To be able to put simple machines together, or to change a battery, or to understand the toaster and the way the lawn mower and clock works is part of what we need to do in life.

"I need a head of lettuce."

Bev - A child walked in to school and, not even entering the school proper, he leaned against the door jamb and said, *"I need a head of lettuce."*

I asked, *"What kind?"*

He said it didn't matter. I immediately sent a parent to the store for lettuce. The child waited in the hallway of the school for the lettuce. He put the lettuce in a large bowl and then asked for milk, which he poured over the lettuce. He added food coloring and mixed it all for a few minutes. He then asked to microwave his concoction.

I asked, *"How long?"*

He said he would come with me. After microwaving his experiment for a few minutes he played with it and examined it with a magnifying glass.

Then he put it in a plastic bag to take home. His dad called and asked, *"What in the world is this?"* As gently as I could, I explained that it was his son's experiment for the day. I made the dad promise me he would always support this child's inquiring mind.

Part of setting up the environment is having lots of loose parts and making space for children. Soon after the school term starts, as I become acquainted with the idiosyncrasies of the children, I ask myself each morning, *"Do I have everything Gracie needs?" "What about Arul?"* Then as the children develop and interests change I must continue to put out different materials. I watch and listen to the children for clues.

. . . as I become acquainted with the idiosyncrasies of the children, I ask myself each morning, "Do I have everything Gracie needs?"

- Bev Bos

Fan with a plastic tube – child is adding feathers and confetti

The sandpile, that simple pile of sand in a place it's not supposed to be (except for here in this place) provided the longest period of exploration this year. It's a beautiful thing.

- Love, Gregg

For parents, it is knowing what their own child loves to do and where to find science, art and music, story and playscape ideas. Both Jenny and I find the more we play with "stuff," the more ideas we have. The more you watch children, the more you understand what they love to do. One of the traps I witness so often is that parents, for birthdays and holidays, purchase the latest television-driven toy or gizmo without considering their child's real interest.

So I decided on 3,000 pounds.

<u>Bev</u> - While observing the school of a friend and teacher in Ohio, she told me she had brought quite a lot of sand inside her schoolroom this year. It had been a long winter and the children missed being outside. Although we go outside rain or shine, I had to see for myself what would happen if we brought lots of sand into the school. Deciding how much sand was impossible, so I decided on 3,000 pounds. It seemed enough and yet not too much. I moved two tables that we used everyday for clay, science and puzzles,

to the rug area and dumped all the sand in a big pile. It is important to know that although our whole yard is sand, dirt, water and gardens, you would have thought these children had never seen sand before. They rolled in it, dumped, poured, patted, shoveled and made sand angels for hours. All of them played in it.

Of course, there was resistance from skeptical adults! One of the teachers threatened, halfheartedly, to withdraw her services. She watched long enough to see the power of sand play in a non-traditional space and decided to stay. Adult helpers stood by with brooms and shovels, keeping the mountain of sand in place. When it was time for the sand to disappear, we gave each child a bucket. The sand was moved outside in about twenty minutes.

At the end of the school year, a father wrote this in a note: *"The sand pile, that simple pile of sand in a place it's not supposed to be (except for here in this place) provided the longest period of exploration this year. It's a beautiful thing. Love, Gregg."*

The unconventional location for the sand was new for the children. It heightened interest and changed the way children used it. The brain responds positively to new sensory 3D experiences. An environment that is static, having sand in only one location, does little for firing up neurons.

Sand under the bed.

Bev – A young mother living in Maine, knowing her child needed to play with sand, no matter what the weather, built a large box on casters to store under the bed and filled it with sand and sand toys. She would wake to the sound of that box being rolled out in the morning. She told me she had a lifetime to have the floor refinished and he had only a short time to be a child. This may be his strongest and most enduring play memory.

Sand is an important element for a whole range of reasons and people. Sand slipping through an egg timer mimics the first clocks made by humans. The quality of this material lies in its power to satisfy everyone from the Japanese master sand gardener to the baby with a metal spoon and cup playing in the washing-up tub filled with this golden, grainy, gritty, galvanizing, gorgeous, ground rock.

In large spaces or small spaces, sand is an inexpensive, long lasting, intriguing play material. Ideally the pile should be enormous, covering acres of hot, inhospitable asphalt. In reality sand sometimes has to be provided in a more limited form. Sand can be put in a small wading pool inside or outside. Most sand tables are not deep enough to hold sufficient sand for deep digging that is the only thing that satisfies a digger mining to China.

Look for large barrels, plastic or wood, and cut them to size, smooth or tape the edges and fill with sand. Have lots of them; one will not do. A galvanized horse watering trough works very well but it would be better to have two or three.

Water is another important element to explore. It is essential to provide water play everyday for young children as a part of your science curriculum. It is both calming and

exciting. Water runs away, can be poured, scooped, spilled, captured, pumped, it can flow and it can be stopped. It changes states from solid to liquid to vapor.

You will most likely not be able to have a lake or a river running through your yard, so the hose and numerous containers must suffice. Remember to elevate some of your containers and lower others so the water is able to flow. Small tables and milk crates provide footings for water tubs. Do not fuss about children getting wet; just have clothes for them to change into if they want to. Children rarely catch colds from being wet or cold.

"It's empty!"

Bev –A visiting seven-year-old ran up to me with a huge funnel and said, *"It's empty."*

I looked inside the funnel and said, *"Yes, there's a hole in the bottom, all right."*

He repeated his statement. I took him over to the water and had him put the funnel in a big container and pour colored water through it and encouraged him to watch the water run through the funnel. He just didn't have any experience with funnels. It made me feel very sad.

Buckets, shovels and scoops.

Jenny – The organizers of the Vancouver Children's Festival, with a stroke of genius (from the viewpoint of a young child), had seen fit to dump a few truckloads of sand in the public park where the festival was being held. A toy storeowner had donated buckets, shovels and scoops. Parents gathered around the edge while the children were enthralled with this chance to play with sand. Parents tried to coax them away to go to the shows. After all, tickets had been purchased in advance and some of the adults grumbled about having spent money on tickets when all the children wanted to do was play in the sand pile!

Age and stage was irrelevant. Everyone was digging, shoveling, pouring, sifting and reveling in the joy of access to a huge mound of sand. It is not difficult to procure a load of sand, but it was cleared away at the close of the festival. The flat grass appeared again for the lawn mowers to keep tidy and clipped leaving the children's intense activity and pleasure a distant memory.

Most of all, science is fun and breathtaking for young children. Science engages children in a process that builds critical thinking skills and the ability to solve problem. It encourages lifelong learning.

The following is a beginning list of loose parts for science. Keep the list handy and expand on it. Once you start looking and collecting you see the world of useful things for science differently. You begin to develop a different way of thinking. Our intention was not to make this a "how-to" science chapter with a gazillion experiments. Instead we have included some of the ones where we have witnessed keen interest and where children extended the enterprise far beyond the adult's limited view. We have included the following pages to offer a sampling of the science activities and projects that occur at the Roseville Community Preschool.

Science Supply List

Buckets
Plastic tubes
Rubber tubes
Funnels and cones
Liter bottles (cut in half w/ edges taped)
Tubs
Smooth plastic gutter (various lengths)
Rocks
Clay pots
Bamboo (both wide and narrow)
PVC pipe (various lengths)
Old-fashioned water hand-pumps
Rope
Old pots and pans
Insulation pipe (cut in half horizontally)
Sticks, stones and bones
Bowls
Milk cartons
Plastic containers
Clear plastic pipe
Boxes
Film canisters
Spoons and shovels
Colanders
Wooden spoons and scoops
Sifters and sieves
Juice cans
Hose
Spray bottles
Ice cube trays
Turkey basters

Most of all science is fun and breathtaking for young children.

*Ice
Sculpture*

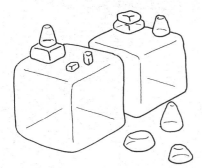

ice, salt, food coloring

pushing pencils through a
sandwich bag of water

*Wood trim moulding for
ramps and inclines*

plastic bottles
& wading pool

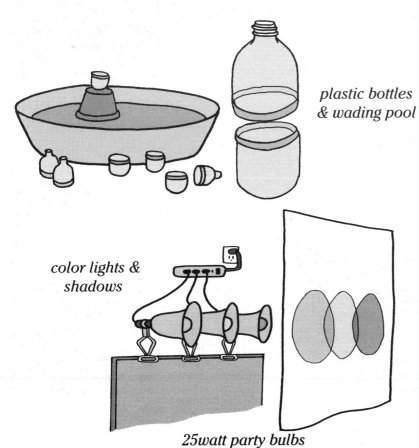

*color lights &
shadows*

25watt party bulbs
red, blue, green

A "Real" Air Project

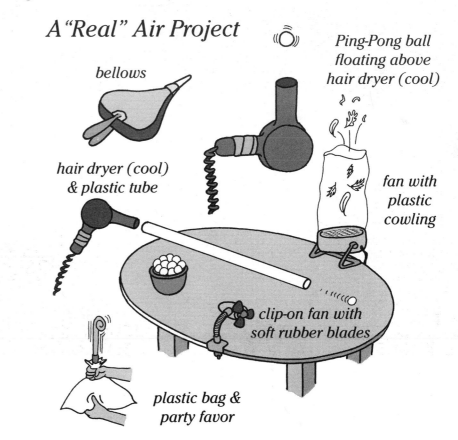

bellows

*Ping-Pong ball
floating above
hair dryer (cool)*

*hair dryer (cool)
& plastic tube*

*fan with
plastic
cowling*

clip-on fan with
soft rubber blades

plastic bag &
party favor

Chapter Eight

BLOCKS

Build it Up and Knock it Down

The cores of cities, ancient and modern, house the edifices that mankind has built throughout the centuries, one technique displacing another as the buildings reach for the sky. We still are puzzled as to the mathematical and construction skills of the builders of Stonehenge, the Pyramids and the Mayan temples. Everywhere children begin building, they use stones, tree limbs, sod, bricks, sticks and blocks of wood that they find in their environments.

The lowest common denominator of blocks in preschool is the standard set of blocks. Although these are excellent tools their limitation is that there is rarely enough with respect to number and variety. There could never be enough blocks for children. Consider the math; a parent would purchase for their child a complete set of blocks, therefore doesn't it hold that a classroom with twenty-five children should have a million blocks? In workshops with adults we will limit their small groups to one hundred blocks and in no time at all they are searching for more.

Blocks provide opportunities for children to practice emerging skills such as sequencing, balancing, sorting, patterning, grouping, building horizontally, building vertically and designing. Children often gravitate towards blocks, a favorite prop for mathematical, imaginative and dramatic play.

A good friend collected a large basket of off-cut wooden pieces and her children used them to build with for years. Her children are in their teens now but the blocks are still there for visiting children. They always provide a focus for action and attention.

Balancing, sorting, classifying, patterning, adding to, taking away . . .

All my own work.

Storage is important for easy access. Our blocks are stored and sorted into boxes or plastic crates. There are those that insist block be kept on special shelves with an outline so each block goes back into its proper place. Some children will opt to do this but it is important that the issue of storage not interfere with the play value. When children played alongside working parents in gardens, fields, forests, riversides and the children had unfettered time to experiment with natural materials. Blocks should be taken outside. The bigger picture here is that genuine construction takes place outside. Block play confined to a small corner of the child's space is a token attempt at honoring the scope and importance to children of block play.

The pleasure and intensity of a child crafting a structure with stumps and stones, twigs and shells can only be found if we have adults willing to take the loose part paradigm to unconventional dimensions. Once you start looking for things to build with, the horizon broadens. Milk cartons, driftwood, tongue depressors, film canisters, stones, spools, PVC pipe of various lengths (with fittings), the list is endless. One of the things we recommend parents do is to take their child to a recycling center and let them browse – filling up a bag with stuff.

<u>Bev</u> – We have a large basket of assorted colored stones, which occasionally decorates our large dinner table. We put fifteen or twenty stones at each place setting and immediately upon sitting down, the old and the young and the in-betweens cannot resist the chance to play and make patterns. They stack, move, line up and trade the rocks, staying at the table long after the meal is finished.

<u>Jenny</u> – A friend had her ten-year-old granddaughters visiting. The granddaughter asked, *"Granny, have you any blocks?"* The grandmother rummaged in the basement and found a box of assorted blocks that had belonged to

her own children. On a desktop, the granddaughter laid out a floor plan of a house and then spent hours making dolls and furniture out of paper. Never throw your blocks away.

When children play with blocks alongside another player it becomes contagious. They discover other ways of using blocks by working with and observing each other. Try putting a set of Dr. Drew's Blocks®, Kapla Blocks® or Tree Blocks® out on your coffee table at home and notice when you have company how most adults just cannot keep their hands off them.

A refrigerator full of blocks.

Bev – Our blocks are kept in sturdy milk crates. A child once hauled a full crate of blocks up to the loft and placed all of them on the shelf of the child size toy refrigerator. There were at least one hundred small wooden blocks, all uniform in size. The arrangement the child made with the blocks was symmetrical as he tucked each of them into the refrigerator. Unfortunately, an adult finding the blocks in the refrigerator assumed it was the wrong place for them and cleared the blocks away.

How quickly we forget! Children need to move things, take them apart and try to put them together and fit things into different spaces. It is how they figure things out. I understand the need to straighten up but we lack sensitivity when we follow a rigid clean-up routine.

In order to understand the concepts related to dimension, children must work in three dimensions. A computer-block building program for young children is useless because it lacks tactile experience or the opportunity to work in three dimensions. Children need to build their constructions up and knock them down and then build them up again. They must touch, talk about, take apart, change, manipulate and

100

Blocks

Hexablocks®
Dr. Drew's Blocks® (one of the best blocks
   for families)
Kapla Blocks®
Standard wooden blocks – at least two
   sets
Hollow Blocks
Tree Blocks®
50 pine 1 x 4 planks (24- and 30 inch
   lengths)
Spools
Furniture legs
Cardboard tubes
Film canisters
Masonite
Look in recycling centers for plastic cut
   offs (we have hundreds of pieces to
   build with)
Duplos®
Lincoln Logs®
Tree rounds
Tongue depressors

(In a home setting the volume of blocks
will have to be adjusted for the available
space.)

"I just don't think a dozen eggs is going to be enough?"

build on yesterday's block play in order to lay a foundation for a higher level of understanding, especially mathematical.

Build a wall, build a wall.

<u>Bev</u> – It is a tradition to bring hardboiled eggs to school to color. We bring them in September, October and as often as I can remember to do it. The children in the school would do this every week. I bring, at least seven-dozen eggs, so I know there will be enough for everyone to color, thus the frantic behavior, the grabbing, the whining and the tension is lessened. We set this up by putting a thick terry cloth cover on the table to minimize the frustration for everyone. The cloth soaks up the spills without us having to constantly flap about with rags or a sponge. We use a strong solution of food coloring or liquid watercolor and water as our egg dye.

After the children finish coloring all the eggs, often they color them again. The final result is seven dozen eggs all greenish brown. I whisk them into the refrigerator until just before we gather, usually midway through the day. At that time, I cover the carpeted gathering area with a fabric drop cloth on which I put at least twenty-five different things with which to build. As the children gather I say, *"Build a wall! Build a wall!"*

After they have been building for a while I bring out the seven-dozen eggs and in my most dramatic way I chant, *"Humpty Dumpty sat on the wall. Humpty Dumpty had a great fall."* The children place the eggs on their walls and sometimes the eggs fall off the walls or the children knock them off themselves. Some children focus on rebuilding their wall so as to help balance the eggs. Occasionally, they help each other to make nooks and crannies to support the eggs. Not all children get involved with the building; two or three of the children may just eat the eggs and a few others are onlookers.

Children find a place to build in this tight space, choose what they want to build with and sometimes search for more of what they need. In doing so, they demonstrate their power to make decisions, solve mathematical problems using concrete materials, work out physical challenges and engage in discussions. The conversations are lively as they figure how tall and how long their structures can be and how many eggs they can balance.

What great physics.

Bev – I planned to color eggs in the spring just before the spring break, but thought since we "do" eggs (Humpty Dumpty) many times during the year, most of the children would not be interested. It would probably be a project for only a few of the children. We had about six-dozen hard-boiled eggs and I put them on a table with containers of food coloring, spoons and trays with soft towels to dry them. The first five children in the door quickly colored a few eggs and then scampered outside with the eggs and put them on the wooden water trough connected to the hand water pump. There, they watched the force of the water push the eggs into a container they placed at the end of the trough. When I witness things like this I can't help but think; what great physics!

Several of the children colored a dozen eggs and ran outside to hide them. They never looked for them and I suppose a stray animal ate them over spring break. Two or three more children colored a few and then ate their eggs. While I turned around to help a child, another child quickly got the shaving cream and removed the color from a dozen or so eggs and then colored them again. One child put half a dozen eggs into a bag saying, *"I need them for home."* All of a sudden there wasn't a single egg left. Why do I ever try to predict what children who have been encouraged to explore, think, wonder and play will do?

"Is it all it can be for every child?"

<u>Bev</u> – On another occasion, the eggs were colored again, but from observing, listening and thinking about children and their needs I changed how I structured the Humpty Dumpty experience. Instead of putting the eggs into the refrigerator and waiting until gathering time an hour and a half after the coloring of the eggs I put out the twenty-five sets of blocks and other building stuff for Humpty Dumpty right away. The children dashed in, colored the eggs and went directly to the carpeted area and started constructing, putting together the blocks to cradle and balance the eggs.

Initially, the teacher defined the time frame for this experience. We traditionally gather toward the end of the

session before we go home. It really limited the time that the children could extend, experience and persist in this play. Our observations of the children led us to change the time frame. Sometimes it is so difficult to see things in a new way, especially when the old way has been successful. When we did the building and balancing separately it was captivating just as it was. But I thought, *"Is it all it can be for every child?"* Often it is easier to continue to do something the way it has always been done in the past. It is hard to take the risk to change what feels safe and try a new way. Despite resistance, I planted my feet and my heart in risk and experimentation and insisted that we try another way.

Later.

<u>Bev</u> – The following story is from a co-teacher. She spread out the canvas drop cloth, put out the blocks, and gave the new way a try. A tribe of boys ran into the school and headed toward the door to the yard. Sally, the teacher said, *"We are doing the eggs."* They, in a chorus, said *"Later."*

The few children that remained inside constructed, built and manipulated the blocks and the eggs all morning long. Some moved in and out of the building area. Finally, toward the end of the day the space was cleaned up, blocks put away and story time started. As Sally sat down to read, the door flew open and the boys ran in and said, *"We are ready to do the eggs now."*

Sally said: *"Well, okay. It will only take a few minutes to get the eggs."*

Quickly, the adults move into action, laying the canvas down and getting the eggs, and everyone became involved in the building again.

All of us probably have some insecurity, some hesitancy about the unknown. It is safe to sit and read a story. Adults need to focus on discovery, going beyond the known. The story time was next. This is not to say that we don't honor the reading or telling of stories, but for the children to extend their drive to know, the teacher must look for the moments when children's enterprise is foremost. The teacher knows that action and play will, no doubt, grab the attention of most of the group. The children trust that their passion and timing is as important as the teacher's project and there is room for both. Another adult could be enlisted to read the story to those children who are interested or, if this is not possible, the story could be delayed. Flexibility is necessary in either case.

The budding scientist.

<u>Jenny</u> – Hard-boiled eggs were in abundance on the art table. This was not a spring or an Easter project, it was early November. The children were dipping them in food coloring. Jeffrey came to take a look at a group of four or five children coloring the eggs. He looked across the room to another table where tall, clear containers of water and oil, part of a science project, were standing. Jeffrey took a colored egg over and asked for the shaving cream, adding about an inch of it to the surface of the oil and water. He placed the egg on top of the mixture and watched as it descended very slowly through the layer of cream. It emerged having lost most of its bright purple color. What was happening here? The budding scientist repeated his experiment. He removed the color from lots of the eggs and engaged several other children in the adventure.

What is interesting to me is that in some other places Jeffrey might have been discouraged from moving this activity into the unknown. The known was coloring eggs and the new frontier was Jeffrey's discovery.

"It's my wall!"

Bev – When planning, I try not to have a preconceived notion about how children will use the materials. I put the child's curiosity and need to explore the materials in their own way before convenience, order or clean-up. I did not know shaving cream would remove color from eggshells. This was Jeffrey's experiment, his discovery, but I also learned something new. This experiment has not happened since. But other spontaneous instances of science play have occurred in the school.

A space where block structures can be left up and revisited, rebuilt and renovated over a period of time, for days or even weeks, is desirable. Every new home built should have a block room. It is with absolute horror that we hear of video game rooms, television rooms and computer rooms while no space is given to one of the most fundamental materials a child could ever be given – blocks.

"Can I use that hammer when you are through?"

Chapter Nine

RICKY'S ROOM

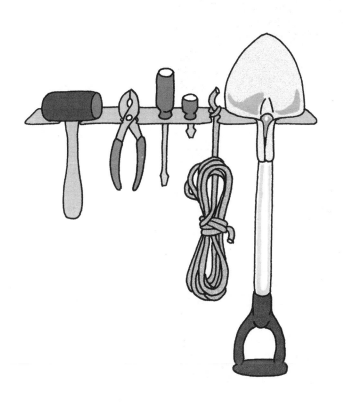

A few years ago, a young boy died while he and his family belonged to the community of our school. Ricky was a child who loved mechanical things, always taking apart and tinkering with everything. He especially loved to fiddle with the family's automatic garage door openers, opening and closing them over and over, wearing out many. His parents understood that wondering how things worked was his passion. They knew other children needed the opportunity to delve into this kind of exploration.

The parents came to me with the idea of building a small room for mechanical exploration. So, with the memorial money in hand, we started. They had much more of a plan than I did and I let them take the lead. Some of the most important changes happen at the school when I pay attention to my heart and trust others with an idea. From the beginning we called it "Ricky's Room" and today I am sure many of the parents involved in the school have only a vague idea why but accept that we must have a reason.

What an absolutely incredible room for the development of mathematical and spatial intelligences! As I watch the young children working in Ricky's Room I can imagine these children in twenty years. There, one can see the mathematicians, scientists, engineers, artists, surgeons, cabinetmakers, electricians and also lawyers. We have become too dependent upon "the experts" to solve all of our mechanical breakdowns. Hopefully, these children, boys and girls alike, will have some practical wisdom of their own to rely on.

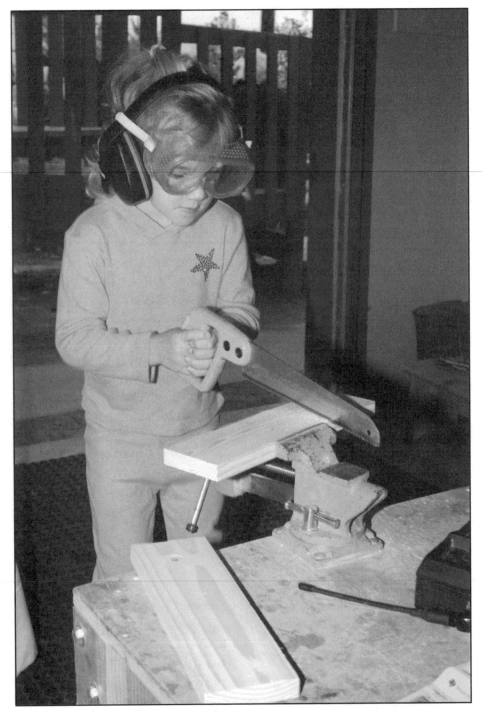

Working hard at work worth doing.

The room is painted gray, with black and yellow trim, and looks like a real workplace. It is a place in which to take things apart and sometimes to put back together. There is a wooden car with real seats that faces a window looking out into the school's play yard. Children love to sit in that big wooden car going nowhere except in their imaginations.

Wooden workbenches with vises hold wood for drilling with hand drills. One wall is painted with blackboard paint and chalk is nearby for drawing plans for this project or that. The benches are often covered with take-apart things: small motors, old typewriters, irons, toasters and mixers (with the cords cut off) that provide hours of work removing screws, bolts and other various parts. The parts they take off are put in heavy-duty plastic bags to be taken home.

Small wooden lockers hold goggles, work aprons and hard hats. One of the first lessons for adults is to help the children clamp down their work. This frees up both of the children's hands. A Peg-Board holds some of the tools and a huge piece of sheet metal holds the magnetic things you might need. Other tools like drills and saws, hammers and nails are kept in a locked cabinet and these are dispensed by the adult assistant.

Part of the floor and wall is covered in fatigue mat (restaurant supply businesses have them) where children can build geometric shapes out of PVC pipe and fittings. Some pretend they are building skyscrapers and with old sheets draped over the top they live in their buildings.

Like everything else in the school, this room is constantly evolving. As families join the school community, new ideas and passions blend with the existing environment. Throughout the evolution of Ricky's room, the woodworking area has expanded tremendously.

Here is a smattering of woodworking ideas:

In the backyard, the old tree stump or a log with some roofing nails and a rubber mallet are a starter set for a carpenter. We have palm tree stumps at school that are just right for pounding roofing nails into with a rubber mallet. The stumps are porous and fairly easy to pound into. One of the stumps, three feet in diameter, is completely covered in roofing nails.

The children soon progress to using claw hammers, (scaled to their size,) screwdrivers, measuring tapes, saws, C-clamps, and hand-crank drills. And yes, there are safety goggles, too, and adults standing close to assist, to remind and fetch.

There is a 12 foot long child-height workbench in our woodworking area. It is big enough for ten children to work around. It is covered with layers and layers of glue and paint and it is still one of the most beloved places to play in the school.

One child may be interested in putting glue on wood pieces. Another will add small pieces of wood to the glue. A third

might be nailing or sawing. Again, it is the process, not the product that is of paramount importance.

The simplicity of wood and a child's delight in having the opportunity to play and work with it encourages them to return many times to build. The material often stays the same but what children do with it varies. Each glued or hammered-together work of art is unique.

Adults struggle with finding gifts for our children on holidays and birthdays and sometimes fail to remember that the simple materials, "real things," can be the truest treasure.

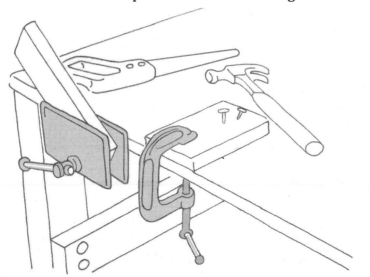

Woodworking Supplies

Masonite – 12" x 14" rectangles
Offcuts – leftover pieces of ply or chipboard
Lots of small pieces of wood for gluing / nailing
Small wooden spools
Soft pine offcuts
C-clamps and vises
Assorted pieces of tile
Wood curls
Nails
Hammers
Paint
Glue
Sticks
Saws
Handheld drills
Brushes
Screws
Sandpaper
Palm sanders
Emeryboard
Sponge sanders

Chapter Ten

GARDENS AND GARDENING

"Every child should have mud pies, grasshoppers, water bugs, tadpoles, frogs, mud turtles, elderberries, wild strawberries, acorns, chestnuts, trees to climb, brooks to wade, water lilies, woodchucks, bats, bees, butterflies, various animals to pet, hayfields, pinecones, rocks to roll, sand, snakes, huckleberries, and hornets; and any child who has been deprived of these has been deprived of the best part of . . . education."

– Luther Burbank

Children feel drawn to the earth, to fresh air, to grass, to flowers, to soil and to watching sow bugs, spiders and ants. Before the children are sidetracked into the world of toys and products, they demonstrate a fascination with anything that is alive and growing. Even in the most inhospitable places children will find a way to connect with nature; robust in their encoded message to thrive in the natural world. The task of the adult is to honor this natural inclination by making sure earth spaces are preserved for children.

Another example of how adults tend to get things out of order for children is by they asking them to be responsible for remote and abstract problems such as rainforest preservation. These programs risk creating an overwhelming sense of fear by forcing children to cope with situations both out of their control and beyond their ability to reason. We first need to help create an intimacy between children and their own backyard – their immediate natural world.

Look closely at your home, roadways, boulevards, sidewalks and the odd neglected corners along the railroad tracks and at the edges of schoolyards and playgrounds. This is where you will find a patch of abandoned or

Getting ready for spring planting, Zac was holding two hands of earth rich in humus and he said, "You know, Grandma, I think if you don't do this when you are young you won't know how to do it when you are older."

forgotten earth and children digging and scraping in it. The children's interest is captured by what they find in the earth, the worms, the centipedes, the sow bugs, the snails and beetles.

Creepy crawlers.

<u>Jenny</u> – In Boston, Massachusetts, a community group were reclaiming space in the city for gardens. One Sunday families came to plant bulbs in a discarded orchard area that had been, in recent years, encroached upon by the city. Two boys, about seven years of age, were given trowels and bulbs. The earth was tough to dig, but they persisted, ignoring their initial task of planting bulbs but totally engrossed in investigating the dormant larva of the coddling moth and, of course, the earthworms that existed underground. They were so excited. I suspect it was the first time they had discovered these creepy crawlers.

Children focus on what interests them and we need to provide tools, time and mentoring for them to do so. The tools for young children are old spoons (wooden and metal), discarded containers, sieves, strainers and old pots and pans. After children have had time to play in the earth, they will be ready for gardening. Make sure you provide tough gardening tools such child-size shovels that are sharp enough to shift earth, rakes with prongs that collect the rocks and do not buckle, trowels that fit a child's hand and watering cans with roses (perforated spouts) that sprinkle – not dribble – water. The emergent gardener can use these tools.

Planting is the time when lots and lots of seeds have to be on hand. Go no further than your kitchen shelf where dried beans, peas, wheat berries, lentils and alfalfa seeds will all sprout in profusion. Start saving seeds from everything and use them the following year.

Put your saved seeds in resealable plastic bags and keep them in the freezer until you want to plant them. When they are dry, you can put them in labeled jars so that you will know what you are planting. If you don't label the jars just plant them freely and be surprised.

Even if the cost of seed is not an issue for you it is important that children see the complete growth cycle from harvesting the seeds to planting them the following year in the garden.

The cycle should start with the maintenance of a compost pile. If you are in a place where winter freezes the poor little red wigglers then try indoor worm composting. If this is done correctly there is very little smell.

If you need assistance with any ecological project, seek help at your local gardening store. Universities often staff hotlines dedicated to answering gardening questions with people who are familiar with the local climatic conditions. The elders in any community may have information about gardening as well. I learned from a master gardener that if you remove a hundred pounds of vegetables from your garden plot you better add two hundred pounds of humus in return to the earth.

Look outside under and around trees. Trees are prolific producers of seeds. Some of these seeds will grow and some will not, but don't be disappointed. Just because something was unsuccessful does not mean the experience was not valuable. When you are walking along and you find seeds that are sprouting try putting them in an earth-filled container and watch them grow. Tree seedlings can find a home in a large pot or container to form a mini forest. Put some green growing mini trees on your windowsill before they move outside.

Greening the school

Some of the packaged seeds that you can purchase are scarlet runner beans. These are great climbers and have beautiful red flowers when they bloom. The red scarlet bean seed is also delicious. Other vegetables we have been successful in growing are zucchini, pumpkins, radishes, lettuce and beets. Most of these seeds need a garden box or plot of earth with a depth of twelve to fourteen inches of soil. They also need light, sunshine, water and consistent care to produce results. More and more people seem totally unaware of where their food comes from. It is distressing to find that the people have no idea that the turnip is a turnip and the beetroot is a beetroot.

Strawberry tubs, berry canes and bushes, depending upon your climate, will add to the greening of the space and perhaps provide you with berries to eat. Look for thornless berry plants.

Herbs can provide some of the greatest pleasure as you crush mint, lavender, sage, lemon balm or basil leaves. The smell of crushed marjoram, thyme or bay leaves can be used to fuel a memory. Herbs such as mint can be used to infuse as tea.

Onion sets and garlic are the edible bulbs. They grow so easily and, if you let them go to seed, the flowers are just lovely. Although crocus, daffodil and tulip bulbs are toxic if eaten, they can be grown for their beauty. It is a personal decision. Some argue the importance of children learning to discriminate between edible and inedible plants despite the potential danger.

Dandelions and buttercups are the toughest of the wildflowers. We often disregard the stunning flowers so-called weeds produce. Get down close to a dandelion and there is no greater beauty. If they were rare they would be prized.

Easily grown plants, flowers and vegetables

Marigolds
Scarlet runner beans
Sweet peas
Clump bamboo
Jasmine
Lavender
Honeysuckle
Verbena
Sunflowers
Radishes
Carrots
Lamb's ear
Hollyhocks
Coreopsis
Wildflower seeds
Buddleia
Thornless blackberries
Blueberries
Snapdragons
Rudbeckia

(Most important is to plant herbs because children can taste and smell them.)
Oregano
Thyme
Basil
Mint
Parsley
Dill
Tarragon
Chives
Sage
Rosemary

Spot-gardening

Sunflowers, cosmos, marigolds and poppies are a few flowers that will give you good returns. If you want more consistent results, buy the seedling plants from a garden center. Fill any old container with soil – making sure there is drainage in the base (holes for excess water to escape) – and plant a mass of flowers to cheer up the most drab and lifeless spaces.

As you garden more and more you will become wiser and choose to plant the framework of the garden space with bushes, vines and shrubs, which do not need replanting every year (perennial). Summer jasmine, honeysuckle, butterfly bush and grape vines are a few such perennials.

Vines have a three-year start-up time. During year one they sleep, through year two they creep and then in year three they leap. So be patient; do not pull vines because they may be sleeping.

Not all places where children spend their days have the luxury of a space in which to grow plants, flowers, fruit trees or vegetables. There are, however, a trillion solutions if you look around. Tubs can be fitted onto carts that can be rolled out during the day and back in at night. Look for one or more of those flatbed dollies or carts on which to place containers filled to overflowing with "alive" earth and plants from dwarf fruit trees to roses to strawberries to beans. (Remember to look out for the giant at the top

Jenny's Mum, Edith Yardley

of the beanstalk!) If you live in an area where the planters could be vandalized, they can be rolled inside at night.

Plant grass seed in any flat container and watch it grow, having children trim it with scissors at intervals. Remember that smell is one of the five senses highly developed in young children so when selecting what to plant, look for fragrant flowers and herbs, such as lavender, basil, marigolds and garlic.

Members of the Earth's battalion.

<u>Jenny</u> – My mother, Edith Yardley, who is ninety-three years old said that she could identify with the need for a child to smell and touch a growing plant. She remembered her own city childhood in Birmingham, England, a heavy industrial city, and the ache she felt for the smell and touch of English bluebells and wild daffodils which they found once a year when they escaped from the confusion, noise, dust and heat of the city.

The gardening experience is one of the most powerful ways in which children can explore all areas of science, art, math, health, social studies, language arts and music. But much more than that, young children become members of the Earth's battalion a mindset that will endure throughout their lives. In a gentle way, children begin to understand the cycle of life, survival and taking care of living things.

No matter where we live, we have to work to take care of the souls of children so that at ninety they will still have trowels in their hands and be planning the planting of the raised beds for the coming year.

Children have the right to be surrounded by beauty.

Chapter Eleven

MOVING

AROUND

Walking is slower,
And not much fun,
Sensible children,
Always run.

It is extraordinary that we attempt to restrict children's movement rather than expand their opportunities to move. Brain research informs us that it is the sensorimotor, child-directed experiences that provide fuel for the development of the brain. We need to help young children broaden their repertoire of movement.

Children need to walk, run, turn, twist, jump, hop, skip, twirl, hang by their arms, roll, crawl and swing in the most natural setting possible so that the patterns for movement and physical prowess are laid down in the brain.

Children, because they are tiny, love to be up high and view the world from a different level. At the preschool we have such places: a loft, a tree house and a ship, but the stairs have been graded, the tree house is enclosed and handholds are available, so we don't have to say, "Be careful!" We know we have made challenging climbing spaces which children can tackle everyday. At first, they go up and down the stairs, sometimes never stopping at the top. It is the climbing, after all, that is important. Then they climb and linger to look out at the view.

Children love to run. However, the directive "no running!" is found in countless spaces where children and adults move around. The statistics, however, confirm that many people, adults and children alike, have low levels

"As children, we are programmed by nature to be little whirling dervishes. Crawling, rolling over, walking, running, skipping, throwing and the like are all intended to form vital physical functions."

- Pete Egoscue

of physical fitness.

When and where does the downward spiral in health begin? It begins in the early years when young children spend more and more of their time corralled in cars being driven everywhere they go. Many children are now living in small dwellings without street level play space and the emphasis in many schools and other spaces for children is on what goes on *inside*. Our ancestors, not so long ago, roamed around often migrating for miles on their feet quickly learning to avoid stumbling and falling. They were constantly having to walk, to run, to dodge, to balance and to twist and turn in their daily lives to survive. They became practiced in the art of movement and if they were to return today they would be amazed to find us with such poor physical prowess.

Keep running.

Jenny – I followed a mother with a small child running ahead of her through an airport corridor. He was about three years of age. She was aware that his ability to avoid bumping into someone else was limited, but instead of shouting for him to look out or stop, she went alongside of him, reached down and took his hand, saying, "Keep running, but we have to make sure we do not bump into people."

There is hope for the human race if more adults would take this tack. We must not prevent children from running but show them how to run with consideration for others.

Skillful skateboarders.

Jenny – One day I watched a young skateboarder skirt skillfully across a busy street, dodging cars and trucks. The parent part of me was a bit anxious. How ironic that he almost fell off his board in shock, when I said to the him, "I am impressed. I wish I had such confidence in my ability to move my body efficiently on a skateboard like that.

We need to provide space for people to move around in diverse ways, not just relying upon motor vehicles. What better way for young people to know and be known in their neighborhoods than to have access to the roadway for their skateboards, Roller blades, feet, bicycles and scooters!

The fear of some accident or catastrophe that leads to litigation has forced adults who live and play with children to narrow the opportunity for measured and necessary risk. What matters to the young child are this second, this minute and *their interest* and not potential lawsuits.

Structures on playgrounds are limited to being four feet high as opposed to increasing the height and building in safety features. Swings are removed, running is discouraged and opportunities for balancing are limited. The climbing ropes are unhooked and gliders are no longer supplied. The result is that children are being shortchanged. They are not given the opportunities they need to practice and take physical risks in their formative years.

In addition to gross motor (large muscle) development that occurs when children constantly move, jump, run, crawl, roll, climb and leap, we need to pay attention to providing endless opportunities for fine motor movement. This is an important factor in brain development.

We have put away our felt pens in favor of wax crayons in all sizes. Felts pens require little muscular effort to scribble or draw. A crayon in the hand of a child exercises the small muscles of the fingers and thumb. Buy lots of crayons and don't discourage the children from peeling and breaking them. Then they can be used as intended: sideways, point first or from the end.

In addition to using crayons to support fine motor development we also have a basket of little wooden spinning tops and we keep looking for different ones. Twisting, turning and spinning the tops are quite a demanding task for small

This minute, this second – that's what's important.

To dig and delve in nice clean dirt, can do a mortal little hurt.
-- John Kendrick Bangs

hands. I marvel at the time children will spend fiddling with these tops.

On worktables we put piles of small rocks, stones and shells to be stacked, rubbed and sorted. Small sets of blocks are placed on the table and pieces of cardboard or index cards are added so children can build in different ways. A pile of sand or dirt is added to the table to build upon. On our light table we put transparent colored plastic chips to be manipulated, moved and stacked, all the while illuminated from below.

In our block area we combine large blocks, small blocks, sticks, stones, balls, inclines, tubes and cardboard gutter – actually any number of recycled pieces – so that children, in their play, must exercise their large and small muscles.

With the best of intentions, parents are enrolling younger and younger children in organized sports and classes. While playing sports may have benefits for the maintenance of fitness for adults, for the young child it is a waste of their precious time. Moreover, the injury level to the body and brain is particularly troublesome because young developing bodies are more susceptible to permanent damage. Injuries sustained when children attempt to copy adult athletic games.

A jillion children.

<u>Bev</u> – The door of the school flings open and in come what seems like a jillion children. Some glance at the art table and a few stop at the science table because they must walk around it to find a path to the back door. Most march through the school and go immediately outside where they can move at will.

If I have learned nothing else in thirty years, it is to trust that a child's brain seeks what it needs to do. It is not an easy thing to do because, unfortunately, most of us have childhood amnesia. We have forgotten how sitting still was torture and how we watched the clock. Ask any child today, "What do you like best about school?" and almost without exception they will say, "Recess!" We may chuckle, knowingly, but they are serious. In the adult world it is the law that offices, courts, factories provide recesses, pauses, respites, and breaks. We deny our children the time to recess, to slip into a quiet space, to let off steam. Recess is also defined as nook, cranny, niche, sanctuary and retreat.

It is time we take them seriously. More and more, recess is being eliminated. How can we justify this? We want our children to have robust health and we must understand this can happen only through a myriad of ways to move in unstructured, spontaneous ways. Ongoing brain research is providing us with compelling evidence that physical movement is part of the foundation of mental *and* physical growth.

"I'm sittin' on the stump with the people I love, telling stories and singing songs . . ."

Chapter Twelve

SINGING TO THE AIR

The thread of lullaby from one generation to the next is quite extraordinary. As the sun goes down and we hold and soothe a child to sleep, we leave in their brain the sounds that bridge one day to the next. Repeating bedtime lullabies to babies and children bonds them to their parents and establishes the pattern for language and provides the hooks to long-term memory. Lullabies are missing for many children now because we seem to have misplaced our own voices relying instead on the technology of taped music.

How do we reintroduce the custom of singing? Sadly, music making in our culture has become more about performance than participation. Is "Happy Birthday" the only song families sing today? There are many moments besides birthdays that deserve to be celebrated with song. The details of people's lives, both the grand and the mundane, need to be etched in song. If we had our way, even the inconsequential moments would be bathed in music – not piped in music – but your voice and the voice of your ancestors, neighbors, children and friends. Imagine the voices of parents filling the grocery store when their children tire or when the stress of the day catches up with them. Someone has to have the courage to start the song. Usually, it is only one person in every family at every gathering that is responsible for keeping the singing alive. It frightens us that this important part of family and society hangs by such a precarious thread.

"Music washes away from the soul the dust of everyday life."

-- Bertold Auerbach

We draw strength from songs. When you are up against hardship and loneliness, down in the dumps or frightened, songs and poetry learned in childhood can calm us and give us the courage to go on. The singing reminds us that times can get better and that we can overcome difficulty. After all, when we sang these songs before, there was an ebb and flow to life and death and singing helped us through those times. When we sing the old songs at funerals and weddings we can reflect on times from the past and shared memories.

Generations share a musical heritage and for the elders, these are the songs that were sung in homes, in schools, in churches, in fields, in gardens and around kitchen tables. When you take the time to sing with elders, you find that if they sang as children the songs stayed with them and can be retrieved, even when the brain appears to be degenerating.   Here is the thread that can connect one generation to another. You don't have to search for the right words to express your feelings, your love, your sorrow or your pain; they are deeply rooted in the songs and the songs take over.

The power of music.

Bev – One night I was talking about the power of music. A young mother shared a story about being out on the ocean when a squall came up and even the captain feared for his life. This young mother didn't know what to do, especially as it was her very first time in a boat. Out of panic came her voice singing nursery rhymes and songs she learned in her childhood. Later, when they finally reached shore, the captain told her he didn't think they would have made it without the songs.

If one is sung to while growing up, songs become a natural remedy during difficult times. In a crisis there isn't time

Blow the wind south o'er the bon ny blue sea.

From this val ley they say you are go ing,

to teach or learn the songs. It has to be a part of your life from the very beginning.

Songs draw people together and resonate with everyone, even when they are sung in an unknown language. The common experience of shared songs gathers us together and helps us to understand the history, the times, the trials and the triumphs of generations past and present. Folk music centers on storytelling, which we know is more easily remembered than any factual account.

Sing the "Onion" song.

<u>Bev</u> – One of my most precious memories of childhood is singing – singing with my mom and dad and three brothers and four sisters. The songs we sang and loved were often not really children's songs but songs passed down from generation to generation. Some were funny, silly songs oft repeated until Mom cried, "STOP!" We sang driving home from Grandma's in snowstorms and the music kept us feeling safe and together.

Everyone had a favorite and most of the time we didn't know the name of the song but asked for it by meaning – "Please, sing the saddle song," which was really "Prairie Lullaby" or "Sing the onion song," which was a song about a "lonely little petunia in a onion patch." Songs said things about love, caring, worries and fears that we sometimes had a difficult time talking about, although many times conversations evolved from the singing.

" . . . let the rest of the world go by."

<u>Bev</u> - It deeply concerns me that families are not singing together as much as they used to. Recently, I was visiting a family and as we sat out in the backyard singing, the grandmother asked me if I knew "Let the Rest of the World Go By" and I sang the song with her. About halfway through

Tell me why the stars do shine,

the song, I glanced at her daughter, a grandmother herself, and she was weeping. Later, she told me she had never heard her mother sing.

Recently in a national weekly magazine, there was an advertisement for a new Minivan that comes equipped with a VCR. The caption suggested this electronic gizmo would change the way children behave when traveling. I know it would not be for the better.   Why would we not see this time as an opportunity to talk or to sing or to invite each other into each other's lives?

If you want to find your voice and bring music to your homes or schools, or bring out the voices of those around you, there are three things about music that are vital that you know. First, music must include children. An invitation at the school is given with a strum of my autoharp and some children come running and others straggle in. As soon as I start the song there is an immediate response from the children: "I've got one!" Most of the time they don't have any idea what song I am going to sing. They just know they will be able to change or modify the song in some way. If colors are part of the song they can change them, or if the song involves movement, the children can add to, change or suggest a different way to move.

I never use recorded music during this time because I know it is always important to sing at the children's pace. Recorded music rarely pays attention to this pacing. Sometimes it does not take into consideration natural body rhythms like breathing or pulse. It does not stop and listen to the stories the children tell as they reveal the connections the songs make to their lives. Some song lines beg to be repeated over and over. Recorded music plows right over and past any opportunity to become more deeply involved as participants and leaves children just trying to keep up.

Most important of all the rules I have for myself, I never use music to teach. A song may have many colors in it, but I would never use the song to stop and "test" whether a child knew the colors or to see how many things were that color in the room. I wouldn't stop a child from noticing that perhaps, "my dress is red," but children are perceptive; they know when they are being tested. The very last thing I want to do is create a condition that discourages children from being involved in music. The more they come to see music as an exercise in trying to guess what I want them to say, the less they will want to make music a part of their lives.

Even more important than the mundane things like teaching colors is the misguided assumption that children can be taught moral lessons with a perfectly crafted verse and chorus about things like honesty, integrity or compassion. We should know better. Children learn these lessons about life from hanging around caring, responsible people. No song ever written can accomplish this.

When we say, *"We learn by heart,"* we are linking emotion and cognition. Rhymes and songs are powerful in that they usually filter into memory through the beat of the heart, the hand, the body and the feet. Chanting, stomping, clapping and dancing are all ways to stimulate areas in the brain, which house memory, motor control, timing and language.

So start singing. If you are uncomfortable, just sing to the air. As time passes you will gain confidence and become less self-conscious. Let the song weave its power and you will be carried away. If you are uncomfortable with your singing voice, start with chants and nursery rhymes. We are a part of the human orchestra by nature's design.

Genre of Songs

Sea chantys
Nursery rhymes
Nonsense songs
Lullabies
Love songs
Goodbye songs
Family songs
Animal songs
Garden songs
Work songs
Chants
Travelin' songs
Campfire songs
Walking songs
Spirituals
Gospel songs
Patriotic songs
Made up songs
Family songs

My grand fath er's clock was too tall for the shelf so it stood nine ty years on the floor,

"Stay close, this is the scary part!"

Chapter Thirteen

PLAYING WITH LANGUAGE

The first babbling and cooing sounds made by babies cause adults to smile, imitate and babble back. This soft rumble of sound tugs at the vocal chords of parents and caregivers. The baby is taking its first tentative steps towards the mastery of speech. This gift of language can best develop through interaction with speaking humans. This is one of the ways children enter into the mainstream of their culture. Before speech, they have to find other ways to communicate. Before becoming articulate, children use body language to express their needs. They point at a particular food or toy. When they do not like something they holler or push the unwanted object or food or person away.

Children need to have experiences to which they attach words. This may appear simplistic and obvious, but it has both significant and profound implications with respect to the development of language. For instance, over the years we have observed children playing with hoses in the yard, the effect of which was erosion on a grand scale. An observer could, at this point, step in and say, "This is erosion!" There is nothing wrong with this, but this is not the most important part of what is occurring. On the other hand, one could trust that the "erosion" experience is now in the child's body and brain, knowing that someday the child will encounter the word "erosion" and *really* know and understand what it means. How less real for the child are having the process of erosion described to the child, or coming across the word erosion in a vocabulary list and being able to use properly it in a sentence.

"One attribute that distinguishes humans from animals is our capacity to tell our own story."

- Laurens Van der Post

The best reading experience – one on one.

Children are often short-changed on language in our society. Consider the hapless children languishing in classrooms where they are expected to produce pat answers. Worse yet is the language diet for the young child that consists of the strident voice of the soap opera personality, the nightly newscaster, the advertisement jingle and the zapped up pace of cartoon-speak and other TV programs. They can easily fall short on time to be immersed in personal and meaningful communication about their lives and the real experiences of their families and homes.

We need articulate, observant, compassionate and courteous people as language partners for children, especially when they are acquiring language. This we know to be true; a child's culture is verbal. They talk about the details of their lives. They talk of things they wonder about and the wonders that they see. For the child these details are relevant and meaningful. All too often we have observed that adults tend to get things out of order. They focus on reading and writing before children have the opportunity to embrace the spoken word. The adult culture demands of children that they sit still, be quiet, and listen. This is especially true of schools where the focus is on performance and scores at the expense of listening and conversation.

"A rich experience of   is an indispensable prelude to literacy. Orality provides a proving ground, a safe place, where a child's imagination can unfold without fear of judgment or censure. Authority and originality hold no sway there; tests and measurements have no place. Stories bring everyone together in a commonality of closely shared knowledge.

But why all the fuss? Why so much attention to what seems so ordinary–to talking and listening? What the big deal about the human voice? The answer

You know why we're so late? We had to take my Mom to the eye doctor. They are going to pull her teeth back there. She didn't drive.

Alana

I am going to live at Yosemite all by myself. I'm going to hike up the waterfalls. And I'm going to live on the waterfalls. And I'm going to tie a rope so I can slide down. And I'm bringing my backpack with lots of snacks. I'm going when my Mom says I can go by myself.

Jacy

Mommy.
Daddy.
Kelsey.
Goldie.
Me.

The end,
Sydney

Storytelling

is simple and direct: Without a full experience in orality a person cannot truly embrace an animating and invigorating literacy. Orality makes social and emotional development possible.

Orality provides the rhythms, the intonations and pitches, the very feelings, that find final expression in writing. Orality thus serves as a preparation – a necessary and powerful foundation – for the construction we call literacy. Children need to hear language in order to learn language."

- Barry Sanders,
from A is for Ox – The Collapse of Literacy and the Rise of Violence in an Electronic Age

Every adult, teacher, parent or grandparent is a storyteller in that we all have a story, our life history. Some people grew up having listened to folktales, parables and myths, family stories that they in turn can share with children. They add to this inventory of stories their own personal and family histories, anecdotes, jokes, tragedies and dramas. These second groups of stories also serve to give meaning and understanding to our lives and, in the eyes of children, make us more human.

Psychoanalyst, Marie-Louise von Franz, believes that stories and fairy tales serve to bring the child's darkest fears and doubts out into the open where they can be discussed. The child no longer feels that only he or she holds a fear of the dark. In the story of the Three Billy Goats Gruff, the Troll is described as an ugly and threatening creature and quite capable of eating goats (and possibly, me!). The goats win out using guile and deception and in the end the Troll gets his comeuppance.

There are many gifted storytellers and there is much to learn from them. And, moreover, there are many books and other resources available for people who may not have grown up in a storytelling culture. Don't forget the importance of finding your own voice. There is an intimacy between child and storyteller when the tale is told. We hope sometimes you will forgo the bedtime storybook and launch into your own tale telling.

Soap Story

<u>Jenny</u> - My great grandfather died when my grandfather was six years old in New Zealand in the late eighteen hundreds. My grandfather and his siblings returned to England on a sailing ship. His mother, a young widow, had a very hard time raising her four children. My grandfather was fortunate to be able to attend school and finally became a doctor.

The story my mother told her grandchildren about her father and the soap sandwich was one she had to repeat over and over again. I am curious to see if that story emerges from their story bank when they have young children. I believe the grandchildren demanded repeat renditions of this story, not just because their grandmother was an expert storyteller but that the tale had links to their ancestor. It had skipped a generation because I have no memory of this story being told to me as a child.

The Story -
It was cold and dark when my grandfather was getting ready to set out for school. The cottage he lived in had no electric light. There was an oil lamp, which was only used

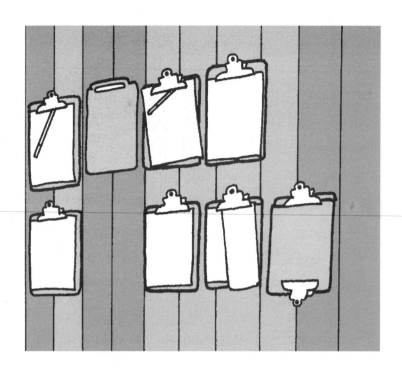

You know what? We went to visit Pa's house. He's in ashes now. The one with the white hair. He's in ashes now. He died.

Holly

"Fee, Fie, Foe, Fum. . . "

in emergencies as they had little money for food and even less for fuel.

His mother, working in the dark, would enter the store room, larder or pantry where food was kept, feel for the loaf of bread, cut two slices and then reach for the cheese. This was his lunch, which he put into his school bag. At lunchtime on the playground, he opened his bag and took out the sandwich. He bit into it and continued to munch when a friend passing said, "Fooks, what is the matter with you? You are frothing at the mouth?" My grandfather pulled his hand across his mouth and found his hand covered with soap bubbles. "Oh, it must have been so dark that my mother found the block of soap and not the cheese!" I believe with boyish bravado he continued munching after all he was hungry and that was the only food he had.

What's that? What's that? . . .

Jenny – I have just spent some time with a four-year-old great-niece whom I had never met before. She trapped me into paying close attention and responding with a constant stream of *"What's that? What's that? What's that?"* This constant questioning is sometimes tedious for adults unless they understand that it is the child's invitation to them to enter the dialogue and take the child deeper into the river of oral language. My great-niece's intention was to seek assistance in her work of building up a collection of words with meaning.

Author Laurens Van der Post has written about the importance of oral stories. He wrote, *"The story was the bushman's most sacred possession. These people knew what we do not: that without a story you have not got a nation, or culture, or civilization. Without a story of your own to live, you haven't got a life of your own,"* and *"One attribute that distinguishes humans from animals is our capacity to tell our own story."*

When telling stories, children naturally interrupt, ask questions, make predictions that spawn endless and unpredictable conversations. The mistake people often make is believing that storytelling is only about listening. Indeed, if we want children to become more articulate, they must have plenty of opportunities to exercise their voices.

Mary Poplin, Dean of the School of Education at Claremont Graduate School offers, *"The single best curriculum innovation we could have to help all students become empowered members of a pluralistic democracy would be to stop the "putting in" of curriculum in the early years and draw students' voices out, listen to their voices, make their voices literate…"*

How does your story start?

In our school we encourage adults to carry clipboards around with them because you never know when some play event may launch a child into a story. Sometimes the story may be the recounting of an experience away from school, something that happened at home, or perhaps, pure fantasy. The adults must be ready to write the story down. When adults honor and respect the child's story, the child will seek out the adult scribe. To be a scribe is to write down a story. The purpose here is not to attempt to teach children to write and read early, but to enrich experience and make the brain connection that writing and reading are core activities in human existence.

We have put such emphasis on the early mastery of print and reading that we have overlooked the recounting of personal experience and narrative.

The princess climbs up to the attic and she gets dead by the sparrows. And then she wakes up and turns into a mermaid. And then the Prince comes to look for her and he said, "Who dived?" and he jumps into the water and grabbed her fin and he pulled her to the surface and she turned human again and she ran…

…away and she got dead again. Then she woke up.

Keevan

Many people today struggle and give up communicating with others because their linguistic foundation is weak. We have put such emphasis on the early mastery of print and reading that we have overlooked the recounting of personal experience and narrative. We must go beneath the skin of language and recapture the essence of children's stories.

Occasionally, we may prompt with, "How does your story start?" The question stated this way invites the child to tell their story. It is important to note that one must trust, implicitly, that the child has a story. To ask the question, "Do you have a story?" implies that there is doubt about the existence of a story.

In their enthusiasm, having recognized the value of recording children's stories, people can get off track. They record private conversations between children or have a conversation with a child (at the puzzle table, for example) and call this a story. The child needs to own the story writing experience from start to finish.

When you first start asking children this question, "How does your story start?" you may have doubts that you can be successful. However, if you just grab a clipboard, pen and paper and find "the talker," (every class has at least one child with the ability to talk endlessly), you will find you are not able to write fast enough, as the child dictates his story. You must be absolutely honest and pure about recording the children's words, as they are spoken – using only paper and pen or pencil. Certainly, there are children that make the connection between the handwritten word and the spoken word during this process and can be observed writing individual letters. But again, this is not the priority. Making their voices literate is.

Do not correct syntax or grammar at this stage. Just write what they say. If the child stops right after the first few

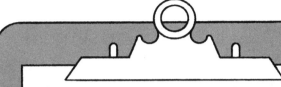

When I am 18 or maybe 21 I can't go here anymore. I have to go to the school by my house.
But if I don't eat food I could go here. But I would die and then I could only go to heaven. Unless my spirit comed here.

Austin

words, don't assume they are through. Pause, wait silently – for at least a few seconds – and then say, *"What's next?"* Or say, *"And?"* Read the story back, off and on while writing, to make certain you have written it correctly. Sometimes when reading the story back, a child will edit the story, adding a piece, deleting or changing it. Do not question this. Remember, this is the child's story. If you change, modify, rewrite or doubt the story you bruise the spirit and undermine the child's sense of self. Here are a few stories scribed from three-, four- and five-year-old children:

My mother is at Boston. She's getting married. She's marrying her friend of hers. She's coming back in five minutes. My dad cooks eggs for us to eat. We eat eggs, waffles and cereal.
Dylan, 4 years old

The princess climbs up to the attic and she gets dead by the sparrows. And then when she wakes up she turns into a mermaid. And then the Prince comes to look for her and he said, " Who dived?" and he jumps into the water and the mermaid swims away. The Prince found her and grabbed her fin and he pulled her to the surface and she turned human again and she ran away and she got dead again. Then she woke up.
Keevan, 4 years old

You know what? We went to visit Pa's house. He's in ashes now. The one with the white hair. He's in ashes now. He died.
Holly, 4 years old

You know why we were so late? We had to take my mom to the eye doctor. They are going to pull her teeth back here. She didn't drive.
Alana, 4 years old

My grandma is a little bit better. (The Grandma had heart by-pass surgery) Her heart was broken. She slept in a doctor's

What frightened me most was that I could have stopped this story from developing to its full potential by making Jeffery work at a different area of the room. How many times do we interfere with their learning?

- Peni Patrick-McArthur

". . . I smell the blood of an Englishman!"

bed. And she got a vitamin. A sun vitamin – just like your earring – to help her heart. She got some of the doctor's purple medicine. Then the doctor gave her some doctor food. He put the food on a flat plate on her bed. It was a peanut butter sandwich. That made her feel better.

Kelsey, 4 years old

I am going to live at Yosemite all by myself. I'm going to hike up the waterfalls. And I'm going to live on the waterfalls. And I'm going to tie a rope so I can slide down. And I'm bringing my backpack with lots of snacks. I'm going when my mom says I can go by myself.

Jacy, 3 years old

My grandpa was at my mom's brother's house, chopping down a old tree. And it fell on his finger. If I was there and I had on my big tennis shoes I would have ran away fast. Because you know how fast I can run. But my grandpa is kinda old and he still can go to work, but he has a bad back and couldn't run away. And my mom has a bad back, too.

Today, he goes to the doctor and the doctor is going to take the stitches out. I don't know if it was a girl or a boy.

My grandma that lives with my grandpa used to be a doctor. I didn't know my grandma was a doctor. She told me. She always tells me safety and I never knew how she knew that.

That big boo-boo sure looked like it hurted. It could of hit the whole thing on him. It's a good thing he's still alive.

Rachel, 4 years old

The stories are collected and placed in a special holder on the wall where we all gather. Near the end of the day, I grab the stories and call to the author of the story. We may make eye contact, but regardless I read the story in its entirety. Most of the time, the only child listening is the

"Marian called it Roxaboxen."

child that dictated the story. I never demand that all the children pay attention. The stories are copied, one sent home and one kept in a folder to be bound and given to the families at the end of the year.

Total regard for the child as a storyteller.

<u>Bev</u> – Tom Hunter, minstrel and music educator, tells of one of his first visits to the school. Having been accustomed to the imposed formality of children being expected to pay attention in any teacher-led group, it took a few minutes of observing to understand what the reading of the stories was all about.

"Bev Bos uses this time to read back the story to the child and to focus on that one child. No one else matters at that moment and, at first glance, this seems chaotic. As I

looked again I did not see disregard for convention but total regard for the child as a storyteller. For those few seconds or minutes it took to read, the child had her undivided attention. What stronger message can a child receive that their work has worth? What better start on the path to becoming a fully literate person?"

"If only someone had asked me my story."

<u>Bev</u> – An observer, a student in education, was visiting one day and watched me read the stories. He got up suddenly and walked away. I found him crying. As I comforted him, he said, *"If only someone had asked me my story."* He had a very troubled childhood and what he needed most was for someone to listen. So often we give children mundane and meaningless topics to write about such as, "Why I like blue ?" or "My favorite food is?"

Parents feel anxious that their children will be ill-equipped to find work as adults unless they have at their finger tips the skills required and valued in the work world. We all strive to help people develop as literate and numerically accomplished adults, but that does not mean that keyboard proficiency, for example, is desirable in a three-, four-, or five-year-old child. Very few people fail to find employment because they cannot use a computer because most adults can, with determination, acquire this skill. The real reason people fail to find and remain employed is because they cannot communicate, solve problems, work with others, tell their story or listen to another's.

Bus Ride

Jenny - It is dark and the journey by bus has been long. The small child sitting behind me is very fractious and the mother constantly tries to shush him. With each attempt to silence him the protests reach a new crescendo. I am wedged into the window seat in front and I am willing the mom to provide some diversion for the child. I am aware that she is getting desperate. After more attempts and threats, she finally dips into the store of memory and begins to tell him the story of the Goldilocks and the Three Bears. She has found the key to helping the little one retreat from the borders of frustration. He is immediately quiet. The pressure to conform to his mother's requests for silence is released and the rest of the adults heave a sigh of relief.

I am not sure why it took so long for her to latch onto the story. But I know that if someone way back in her childhood had not told her that story, she would have been even more agitated and insecure traveling with the child. The jungle from the TV advertisement is no substitute for the age-old rituals of rhymes, stories and poems committed to memory for recall in any number of difficult situations.

"The successful child is not the child who can memorize facts, but rather, the child who can ask the winnowing question."

- Jane Healy

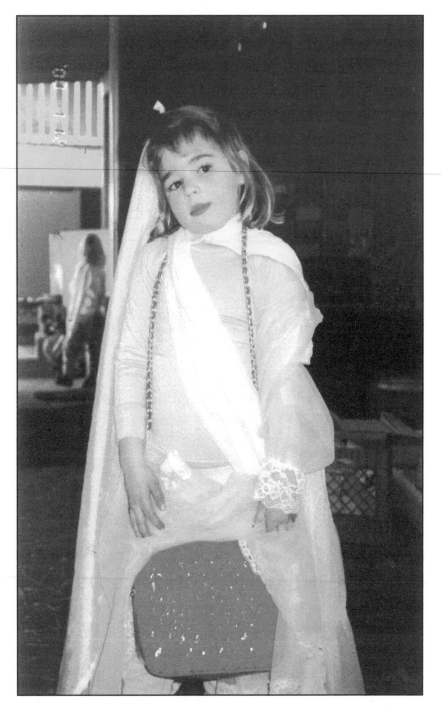

All dressed up and someplace to go.

One friend of mine has carried with her the poetry books from her school days of four decades ago as well as the poems she knows by heart. She recalls that in the darkest moments of her life these poems have been a solace and a straw to hold onto, to give her courage.

Recently there has been a resurgence in exposing children to the old nursery rhymes and poetry. In many cases, these rhymes and poems have been overshadowed by the blast of cleverly crafted advertising jingles. Classes exist for moms and tots to reintroduce them to the timeless Mother Goose rhymes.

"Read it again!"

Bev - One of the things you will notice when you read poetry to children is that they always say, "Read it again." And then they say read another one. I do not hold the book out for them to see as I would do with a picture book. I just read it. Just the other day, a poem had the word red in it and a little boy said, "Red, red, red, bed, bed, bed, dead, dead, dead. Hey, Bev Bos, it rhymes!"

There is something in the rhyming, the chanting and the cadence that resonates with children. If adults have heard the poems as children they are also captivated. There is an immediate image with poetry unlike a book where a storyline must be followed and the sounds are soothing.

Jeffery's Story

Recently, Peni Patrick-McArthur, a teacher with many years of experience, told us her "Jeffrey story" and we asked Peni to write it up and let us include it in our text. We feel it is a universal story and one, which forces us to look at the true value of play and how children launch into literacy.

<u>Peni</u> – This story is about one of those defining moments in your profession when something takes place that has a powerful impact and you know that you have learned and will forever be changed. This story took place about twelve years ago.

Jeffery was a five-year-old in my junior/ senior kindergarten class. He had two older sisters who had both started reading books at the age of five years. Jeffery wasn't reading and his mother was very concerned about this. She came to me one morning to ask me why he wasn't reading yet. I arranged a meeting time with her that would allow me to take the time needed to help her understand early literacy development and where Jeffery was in terms of his reading development. Our meeting was set for later that week.

That morning I began to gather my observations and anecdotal notes about Jeffery's activities at school. I noticed that he had chosen to work at the box sculpture area of the classroom each day for the past week. I went over to him as he was working diligently with boxes, rolls and tape.. I said to him, "Well, Jeffery, you're working hard on something here."

He replied, "Yes. This is my survival outfit!"

The next day Jeffery, again, chose to work at the box sculpture area, and near the end of our activity time he walked into the open area wearing his survival outfit! He had a cereal box on his head with the front cut open to expose his face. He had two wrapping paper rolls taped together as his spear. He had a belt made out of construction paper, a small "Kitty Treat" [cat food] can and at least half a roll of masking tape! Then, on his feet he had made boots from lime green, corrugated cardboard with arrows attached to the sides of his boots. The arrows pointed in the direction behind him. Oh, yes, he also had made a large red circle and taped it to his front, right thigh.

Poems read, poems shed, poems lifted from the page,
Even when the times are dark and people shiver in a cage.
Lights flash on and in our souls,
Words can fill the gaping holes.

- Jenny Chapman

I called out to him, "Hey, Jeffery! Where are you off to?"

He said, "I'm off to the wilderness with my survival gear."

I asked, pointing to his waist, "Is that your belt?"

He replied, "Yup, but not my ordinary belt. You see this can? Well that's my litter can 'cause you are not allowed to litter in the wilderness."

"Oh, I see. And is that your spear?' I asked.

"Yup, I need it because I'll be hunting animals for my dinner," he explained.

"What about your hat?" I asked.

"That's not my hat. That's my helmet. While I'm out hunting for my dinner there will be animals out hunting for their dinner. And you see this red circle? (He points to the red circle taped to his front, right thigh) Well, when I hear something creeping up behind me I just slap this red circle and the arrows shoot out from my boots and gets the animal that wants me for dinner!"

I got my camera and immediately took Jeffery's picture and wrote down every word he had said. This was going to help his mom to better understand and to value his way of learning.

This child had the whole of nature's life cycle expressed in the creation of a survival outfit for life in the wilderness! He demonstrated his understanding of this by working with tape and boxes and paper rolls. This is early literacy. This is the story Jeffery is able to create at five years of age using the appropriate tools. I am sure that later in his schooling, when he had the conventional tools of writing, he was able to put words to paper. Wherever Jeffery is today, I am sure he is writing stories with meaning and depth.

Books

Storybooks and storytelling can take children and adults into lands of fantasy, adventure and wonder. So much of what children come to know these days is through somebody else's pictures. The significance of storytelling is that children are forming their own pictures on the walls of their minds. If children are ever going to be analytical, one of the first steps is to develop an imagination and imagine what could be.

One way we destroy the conversation is by not allowing the listeners to enter the story. The author wants to grab the reader's attention and have a conversation with the reader through the book. For a short time the words and ideas come alive. Do you remember listening to *Peter Pan* and wanting to fly? Every book you read needs to create a desire in the children to be in the story and even to change it and make it their own. In other words, each page must be lingered over, wept over, laughed over or ignored. Children reading or listening to stories inevitably create pictures for themselves in their minds. Having plenty of imaginative experiences as children, however, reinforces and strengthens their imaginations into adulthood.

Books should be under the bed, under the pillow, in the car and in every room of the house to be held, looked at, read and listened to. It is imperative that books remain a counter-balance, if not an outright replacement, to video and television programming.

What follows is an example of what happens when I read a book to my preschool children. Although it is always different, and we constantly share new books, it is hoped that the following illustrates how to read books with young children. Bev – *Roxaboxen*, written by Alice McLerran, is the ultimate story of childhood. It is the story of a group of young children who created the imaginary town of Roxaboxen and was written fifty years after the fact. Roxaboxen describes how through their play the children captured the essence of life, death, continuity, war, protection, town life and community.

In the middle of reading this story to the children, one child said, very quietly, *"We could do this."* And we did. We got hundreds of rocks and made our own spaces. We made cardboard houses furnished with pots and pans and stoves made out of bits stone and pieces of wood and anything we could find. The play went on for weeks as the children sorted out who they would or would not let live in their space.

Tough Boris, written by Mem Fox, is about a tough, greedy, massive, scruffy and scary old pirate, his parrot and a young boy; a stow-away on the pirate ship.

Every time I read this story the responses are different. Last year the children talked about death for twenty minutes. Sometimes they talk about pirates not being real and what is real or not.

The text that follows describes the interactive experience that took place when reading *Tough Boris* to the children.

Page one: "Once upon a time, there lived a pirate named Boris von der Borch."

A child looked at the picture and said, *"He is ugly."*
Me: *"What parts are ugly?"*
Child: *"Every part!"*

Page two: "He was tough. All pirates are tough."

Child: *"My grandpa had a steak that was tough!"*

The conversation continued for five minutes and was about who was tough – my brother and/or my mom.

Page three: "He was massive. All pirates are massive."

I said, *"Massive – hmmmmm?"*
Jeffery: *"Why do you read stories when you don't know the word?"* I really value books that have words I know the children will not be familiar with. I want them to wonder, ask questions or offer their definitions.

Moriah: *"You know, pirates don't exist anymore."*
Me: *"What happened to them."*
Moriah: *"They forgot to get on Noah's ark."*
Me: *"Ahhh!"*

Pirates are scruffy, fearless and scary in this book and each page I read leads to lengthy and profound conversations. Then the parrot dies.

Ally said, *"If my grandpa was here he would cry because he loves animals."*

When we talked about what the pirate was going to do with the dead parrot, so many of the children had ideas.
Alex: *"They are going to put it overboard."*
Jarad: *"I think they are going to dig a hole and bury it."*
Alex: *"They can't dig in the water."*
Sophie: *"I know what they do. They put it in a real hot fire and then they have ashes."*

These are just some of the responses. Then we read the rest of the story and discovered that they put the parrot in the violin case and slide it overboard.

Last page: "Pirates cry, and so do I."

Reading books and stories provides a pathway between the child and reader and draws us closer together. Some children use this time to voice their thoughts, fears and feelings.

For more young children to have the experience of being read to, we need to bring additional readers to their schools and childcare centers. Often, I am asked about the situation of schools being understaffed and short of help. I don't think that we have scratched the surface of the people power out there that is available for reading to young children. Nine- and ten-year-olds can read to

kindergarten youngsters, and can improve the older child's reading skills. So many children are from small families with little experience of older children or teenagers. This provides the opportunity for cross-age contact and the fostering of relationships across age and grade levels.

Some grandparents, given a little encouragement, would be delighted to sit and read for twenty or thirty minutes. The businessperson, on being invited, might give a few minutes once a week on their lunch hour. Parents can be invited to come ten minutes early to school, drop on the rug and read to their own child and others, especially if you provide coffee or tea. The books are ready and waiting to be read.

In all the years I have been teaching, I've never seen a time when there were more good children's books available. I am especially encouraged by the diversity in today's books, socially, culturally and ethnically. I have a list of books that I have used as resource books with success and books that I have read and reread to the children at school and my grandchildren. They are books I am passionate about and will still enjoy in ten years. But to keep the joy of teaching alive for myself and the wonder of learning alive for my kids, I am always on the lookout for that brand new book I can bring in on Monday morning. Our school library shelf is a combination of these two types of books - old loved standards and exciting new discoveries.

Bev - I am often asked why I choose the books I do. While some have suggested I have developed a strong intuitive sense, I prefer to think that I have simply learned from experience. After reading books to young children for more than thirty years, a good book has to meet a certain criteria for me:

• Is it meaningful to the children, something they can make sense of? Does it help them make sense of their world without being condescending? Does it encourage conversations connected to their lives or imagination?

• Is it humorous? Does it promote gales of laughter or heighten a child's sense of fun? Is it, in other words, irresistible?

• Are the illustrations visually pleasing and not overwhelming?

• Does the book encourage children to interact? If it doesn't create conversations by the first page, put it away and get another book.

• Does the story help children toward self-identification or reinforce their self-concept positively?

• Are there opportunities to create – or to expand on the story?

• Is it "preachy," "teachy" or "cutesy"? If so, you are better off without it.

My philosophy is that books do not belong in the library or just on the bookshelf at home. Kids should have easy access to books all the time. At home, they should be under the pillows, stacked by the bed and in every nook and cranny. Every bathroom should have not only newspapers but also children's books. They should be in the car, too.

At school, we make sure the books are within easy reach of the children. Books and words need to be as familiar to children as the food they eat, the music they hear and the art they do. If we want our children to become literate then we must do everything we can to make them comfortable with books and language.

"A real page-turner!"

"Children are watching us live and what we are shouts louder than anything we can say." -- *Anonymous*

Chapter Fourteen

COMMUNITY

Children, parents, uncles, aunts, grandparents, teachers, neighbors

Children are watching us, picking up cues as to how to be in a family, in school, in work, in play and in relationships. The children's heroes should be their parents, siblings, uncles, aunts, grandparents, teachers, neighbors, the school custodian and the postie. These are the people you see and talk to everyday. You must learn what trust is within your family or tribe before you can extend trust and friendship to others. The role models for our children should be people they know personally and not some fleeting image sold as a poster of someone unknown to them, such as a sports personality, a politician, a rock musician or a cartoon character.

We have thrust our children into the whirlpool of adult life too soon. It is our opinion that we have tumbled over the edge. Our culture has subverted the opportunity and the time our children need to grow through childhood and adolescence to join a civil, mature society.

We need to find the courage to question, to swim against the tide, to reintroduce the idea that the journey from babyhood to adulthood involves struggle, resiliency and passion. Individuals must not be cut off from the life affirming joys of adventure, of challenge, of sacrifice and of service to others, which connects them to a sustaining community.

There are a small number of parents who, by design or accident, choose to involve themselves directly in the first years of their child's going to school.

It is our opinion that we have tumbled over the edge.

- Bev Bos, Jenny Chapman

"Corn dogs alfresco, it doesn't get any better than this."

This is often during the preschool period. They may, at the time, enroll in such programs because they have heard some rumor as to the value of their participation and the link between home and the wider world of school.

Suddenly, they are on a roller coaster of parent helping, schedules, meetings, parent work parties and carpooling. At times this seems to be an excessive demand to place upon the parents of young children. They arrive in a community school, and when they find that not only are their children entering an oasis and a place that offers genuine support for each child to play, but they also have stumbled upon a network of other parents who can be friends and supporters for life.

They begin to immerse themselves in the task of understanding childhood, all that exploring, art, science, socializing, running, jumping, swinging, talking, laughing, singing, looking, standing and staring as they begin to understand, they sigh deeply and say, "This is the place for not only my children, but also for me."

There will be no turning back as they become more and more firmly involved in the delights and disturbances of children at play. Here, then is the connection to a vital and growing community of children, teachers and parents striving to make this small speck of a school a truly humane place in which to work and play.

They may not understand fully the lifelong impact upon their families and families' families that being a participant in a community play space will have. This impact is that in the future they will stay connected to children and, through children, to community. They will have strong feelings of hope and awareness of the value of childhood.

"I'm just overcome!"

Bev - A father driving by the school one day this summer noticed that we were in the school yard caring for the gardens. He stopped and backed up to where we were working by the fence. He had dark glasses on and I didn't recognized him at first as he walked towards me. When I recognized him, I put out both hands and said, *"Gee, I'm glad to see you!"* For several moments he didn't say anything at all.

Finally, he said, with tears in his eyes, *"I'm just overcome."*

His children are now in high school and middle school. I had the feeling that he had thought about talking to me someday, and what he might say, how he would express himself, and that after all these years he had realized how important the early childhood years were to his family.

We have watched and listened to the parents, as they have drifted in and out of their helping days, and have developed a deep appreciation of the power of parent participation. There will be much hope for the future if we can infect numerous communities with the spirit we have at Roseville Community Preschool. This spirit is that of a flame passed on from one group to another who has come to trust that their children in this place have had the privilege of joyous childhood experience.

Who cleans up?

CONCLUSION

From quiet homes and first beginnings
Out to the undiscovered ends
There's nothing worth the wear of
*   winning*
But laughter and the love of friends.

- Hilaire Belloc

We have rambled and meandered throughout the field of children's play, intent upon drawing you, the reader, back into the clay of childhood memory. It is our belief that rich childhood play is the only secure foundation from which children should enter into the future. We cannot afford to stand by any longer and allow adults with no real knowledge of young children and their needs to dictate what should be happening for our children. Many of us who work with young children know that something is deeply out of kilter but we feel powerless to effect change. We have to become outspoken and firm advocates for the young child and work to bring about a change of heart in people whose focus is the requirements, guidelines, standards and content for childhood places.

There have been long periods on the evolutionary journey where humans have used their hands and brains to improve their well being. The tools for hunting (the spear), for planting (the digging stick), for sewing clothes (the bone needles), for preparing animal skins (the range of stone scrapers)are examples of this evolution. Up to the present day with communication technology and the harnessing of the force we know as electricity all attest to the vast power of the marriage of hand and head. It is in childhood that such power is first unleashed and practiced.

The fear that our cities and populations will be devastated as the resources of Earth are depleted is real. Yet the capacity of humankind to adjust is still lurking in our genes. We cannot see the solutions to the apparent overwhelming problems for the inhabitants of planet Earth immediately, but we know the ingenious and divergent thinking that surface when we play. It is this that gives us hope for our great-grandchildren. How they flourish and

"Daddy, I don't think I will ever finish my playing."

"I can do it."

thrive, as the next generation will depend to a large extent upon their receptiveness to embracing the unknown and the changes, which are happening all around them.

These children scattered to the four corners of the earth will always know how to renew their spirits when they are dismayed and how to express their enthusiasm when they are joyful. However, we may well tumble over the edge unless we have more people in the mainstream, on the horizon and at the margins of society developing creative solutions to problems as they emerge by relying on cognitive and creative foundations created in childhood.

Our wish is that all of us, parents, teachers, elders, teens and kin can create or find small pockets of hope where children can experience the joy, vitality, richness, pleasure and challenges of unfettered play in their homes, gardens, streets, neighborhoods, parks, schools and schoolyards. These children will then take with them the seed of productivity, support, nurturance and courage throughout their lives.

The end.

Index of Names